QUIT YOUR WORRYING!

GEORGE WHARTON JAMES

1st WORLD
LIBRARY
Literary Society

Quit Your Worrying!

George Wharton James

© 1st World Library – Literary Society, 2005
PO Box 2211
Fairfield, IA 52556
www.1stworldlibrary.org
First Edition

LCCN: 2004195624

Softcover ISBN: 1-4218-0445-X
Hardcover ISBN: 1-4218-0345-3
eBook ISBN: 1-4218-0545-6

Purchase *"Quit Your Worrying!"*
as a traditional bound book at:
www.1stWorldLibrary.org/purchase.asp?ISBN=1-4218-0445-X

1st World Library Literary Society is a nonprofit
organization dedicated to promoting literacy by:

- Creating a free internet library accessible from any computer worldwide.
- Hosting writing competitions and offering book publishing scholarships.

**Readers interested in supporting literacy
through sponsorship, donations or
membership please contact:
literacy@1stworldlibrary.org
Check us out at: www.1stworldlibrary.ORG
and start downloading free ebooks today.**

Quit Your Worrying!
contributed by Tim, Ed & Rodney
in support of
1st World Library Literary Society

TO THOSE

who are standing on the banks of worry before the
ocean of God's love I cry aloud

"COME ON IN - THE WATER'S FINE!"

CONTENTS

JUST BE GLAD

BY JAMES WHITCOMB RILEY

O heart of mine, we shouldn't worry so,
What we have missed of calm we couldn't have, you
know!

What we've met of stormy pain,
And of sorrow's driving rain,
We can better meet again,
If it blow.

We have erred in that dark hour, we have known,
When the tear fell with the shower, all alone.

Were not shine and shower blent
As the gracious Master meant?
Let us temper our content
With His own.

For we know not every morrow
Can be sad;
So forgetting all the sorrow
We have had,
Let us fold away our fears,
And put by our foolish tears,
And through all the coming years,
Just be glad.

FOREWORD

Between twenty and thirty years ago, I became involved in a series of occurrences and conditions of so painful and distressing a character that for over six months I was unable to sleep more than one or two hours out of the twenty-four. In common parlance I was "worrying myself to death," when, mercifully, a total collapse of mind and body came. My physicians used the polite euphemism of "cerebral congestion" to describe my state which, in reality, was one of temporary insanity, and it seemed almost hopeless that I should ever recover my health and poise. For several months I hovered between life and death, and my brain between reason and unreason.

In due time, however, both health and mental poise came back in reasonable measure, and I asked myself what would be the result if I returned to the condition of worry that culminated in the disaster. This question and my endeavors at its solution led to the gaining of a degree of philosophy which materially changed my attitude toward life. Though some of the chief causes of my past worry were removed there were still enough adverse and untoward circumstances surrounding me to give me cause for worry, if I allowed myself to yield to it, so I concluded that my mind must positively and absolutely be prohibited from dwelling upon those things that seemed justification for worry. And I determined to set before me the ideal of a life without worry.

How was it to be brought about?

At every fresh attack of the harassing demon I rebuked myself with the stern command, "Quit your Worrying." Little by little I succeeded in obeying my own orders. A measurable degree of serenity has since blessed my life. It has been no freer than other men's lives from the ordinary - and a few extraordinary - causes of worry, but I have learned the lesson. I have *Quit Worrying*. To help others to attain the same desirable and happy condition has been my aim in these pages.

It was with set purpose that I chose this title. I might have selected "Don't Worry." But I knew that would fail to convey my principal thought to the casual observer of the title. People *will* worry, they *do* worry. What they want to know and need to learn is how to quit worrying. This I have attempted herein to show, with the full knowledge, however, that no one person's recipe can infallibly be used by any other person - so that, in reality, all I have tried to do is to set forth the means I have followed to teach myself the delightful lesson of serenity, of freedom from worry, and thereby to suggest to receptive minds a way by which they may possibly attain the same desirable end.

It was the learned and wise Dr. Johnson who wrote:

> He may be justly numbered amongst the benefactors of mankind, who contracts the great rules of life into short sentences, that may easily be impressed on the memory, and taught by frequent recollection to recur habitually to the mind.

I have no desire to claim as original the title used for these observations, but I do covet the joy of knowing that I have so impressed it upon the memory of thousands that by its constant recurrence it will aid in banishing the monster, worry.

It is almost unavoidable that, in a practical treatise of this nature, there should be some repetition, both in description of worries and the remedies suggested. To the critical reader, however, let me say: Do not worry about this, for I am far more concerned to get my thought into the heads and hearts of my readers than I am to be esteemed a great writer. Let me help but one troubled soul to quit worrying and I will forego all the honors of the ages that might have come to me had I been an essayist of power. And I have repeated purposely, for I know that some thoughts have to knock again and again, ere they are admitted to the places where they are the most needed.

I have written strongly; perhaps some will think too strongly. These, however, must remember that I have written advisedly. I have been considering the subject for half or three parts of a life-time. I have studied men and women; carefully watched their lives; talked with them, and seen the lines worry has engraved on their faces. I have seen and felt the misery caused by their unnecessary worries. I have sat by the bedsides of people made chronic invalids by worry, and I have stood in the cells of maniacs driven insane by worry. Hence I hate it in all its forms, and have expressed myself only as the facts have justified.

Wherein I have sought to show how one might *Quit his Worrying*, these pages presuppose an earnest desire, a sincere purpose, on the part of the reader to attain that desirable end. There is no universal medicine which one can drink in six doses and thus be cured of his disease. I do not offer my book as a mental cure-all, or nostrum that, if swallowed whole, will cure in five days or ten. As I have tried to show, I conceive worry to be unnatural and totally unnecessary, because of its practical denial of what ought to be, and I believe may be, the fundamental basis of a man's life, viz., his perfect, abiding assurance in the fatherly love of God. As little Pippa sang:

God's in his heaven,
All's right with the world.

The only way, therefore, to lose our sense of worry is to get back to naturalness, to God, and learn the peace, joy, happiness, serenity, that come with practical trust in Him. With some people this change may come instantly; with others, more slowly. Personally I have had to learn slowly, "line upon line, precept upon precept, here a little, there a little." And I would caution my readers not to expect too much all at once. But I am fully convinced that as faith, trust, and naturalness grow, worry will cease, will slough off, like the dead skin of the serpent, and leave those once bound by it free from its malign influence. Who cannot see and feel that such a consummation is devoutly to be wished, worth working and earnestly striving for?

If I help a few I shall be more than repaid, if many, my heart will rejoice.

[Signed: George Wharton James]
Pasadena, Calif. *February*, 1916.

CHAPTER I

THE CURSE OF WORRY

Of how many persons can it truthfully be said they never worry, they are perfectly happy, contented, serene? It would be interesting if each of my readers were to recall his acquaintances and friends, think over their condition in this regard, and then report to me the result. What a budget of worried persons I should have to catalogue, and alas, I am afraid, how few of the serene would there be named. When John Burroughs wrote his immortal poem, *Waiting*, he struck a deeper note than he dreamed of, and the reason it made so tremendous an impression upon the English-speaking world was that it was a new note to them. It opened up a vision they had not before contemplated. Let me quote it here in full:

> Serene I fold my hands and wait,
> Nor care for wind, or tide or sea;
> I rave no more 'gainst time or fate,
> For lo! my own shall come to me.
>
> I stay my haste, I make delays,
> For what avails this eager pace?
> I stand amid the eternal ways,
> And what is mine shall know my face.

Asleep, awake, by night or day,
The friends I seek are seeking me,
No wind can drive my bark astray,
Nor change the tide of destiny.

What matter if I stand alone?
I wait with joy the coming years;
My heart shall reap where it has sown,
And garner up its fruit of tears.

The waters know their own and draw
The brook that springs in yonder height,
So flows the good with equal law
Unto the soul of pure delight.

The stars come nightly to the sky;
The tidal wave unto the sea;
Nor time, nor space, nor deep, nor high
Can keep my own away from me.

I have been wonderfully struck by the fact that in studying the Upanishads, and other sacred books of the East, there is practically no reference to the kind of worry that is the bane and curse of our Occidental world. In conversation with the learned men of the Orient I find this same delightful fact. Indeed they have no word in their languages to express our idea of fretful worry. Worry is a purely Western product, the outgrowth of our materialism, our eager striving after place and position, power and wealth, our determination to be housed, clothed, and jeweled as well as our neighbors, and a little better if possible; in fact, it comes from our failure to know that life is spiritual not material; that all these outward things are the mere "passing show," the tinsel, the gawds, the tissue-paper, the blue and red lights of the theater, the painted scenery, the mock heroes and heroines of the stage, rather than the real settings of the real life of real men and women. What does the inventor, who knows that his invention will help his fellows, care about the newest dance, or the latest style in ties, gloves or shoes; what does the woman whose heart and brain are completely engaged in relieving suffering care if she is not familiar with the latest novel, or the latest fashions in flounced pantalettes? Life is real, life is earnest, and this does not mean unduly solemn and somber, but that it deals with the real things rather than the paper-flower shows of the stage and the imaginary things of so-called society.

It is the fashion of our active, aggressive, material, Occidental civilization to sneer and scoff at the quiet, passive, and less material civilization of the Orient. We despise - that is, the unthinking majority do - the studious, contemplative Oriental. We believe in being "up and doing." But in this one particular of worry we have much to learn from the Oriental. If happiness and a large content be a laudable aim of life how far are we - the occidental world - succeeding in attaining it? Few there be who are content, and, as I have already suggested few there be who are free from worry. On the other hand while active happiness may be some-what scarce in India, a large content is not uncommon, and worry, as we Westerners understand it, is almost unknown. Hence we need to find the happy mean between the material activity of our own civilization, and the mental passivity of that of the Orientals. Therein will be found the calm serenity of an active mind, the reasonable acceptance of things as they are because we know they are good, the restfulness that comes from the assurance that "all things work together for *Good* to them that love God."

That worry is a curse no intelligent observer of life will deny. It has hindered millions from progressing, and never benefited a soul. It occupies the mind with that which is injurious and thus keeps out the things that might benefit and bless. It is an active and real manifestation of the fable of the man who placed the frozen asp in his bosom. As he warmed it back to life the reptile turned and fatally bit his benefactor. Worry is as a dangerous, injurious book, the reading of which not only takes up the time that might have been spent in reading a good, instructive, and helpful book, but, at the same time, poisons the mind of the reader, corrupts his soul with evil images, and sets his feet on the pathway to destruction.

Why is it that creatures endowed with reason distress themselves and everyone around them by worrying? It might seem reasonable for the wild creatures of the wood - animals without reason - to worry as to how they should secure their food, and live safely with wilder animals and men seeking their blood and hunting them; but that men and women, endued with the power of thought, capable of seeing the why and wherefore of things, should worry, is one of the strange and peculiar evidences that our so-called civilization is not all that it ought to be. The wild Indian of the desert, forest, or canyon seldom, if ever, worries. He is too great a natural philosopher to be engaged in so foolish and unnecessary a business. He has a better practical system of life than has his white and civilized (!) brother who worries, for he says: Change what can be changed; bear the unchangeable without a murmur. With this philosophy he braves the wind and the rain, the sand, and the storm, the extremes of heat and cold, the plethora of a good harvest or the famine of a drought. If he complains it is within himself; and if he whines and whimpers no one ever hears him. His face may become a little more stern under the higher pressure; he may tighten his waist belt a hole or two to stifle the complaints of his empty stomach, but his voice loses no note of its cheeriness and his smile none of its sweet serenity.

Why should the rude and brutal (!) savage be thus, while the cultured, educated, refined man and woman of civilization worry wrinkles into their faces, gray hairs upon their heads, querelousness into their voices and bitterness into their hearts?

When we use the word "worry" what do we mean? The word comes from the old Saxon, and was in imitation of the sound caused by the choking or strangling of an animal when seized by the throat by another animal. We still refer to the "worrying" of sheep by dogs - the seizing by the throat with the teeth; killing or badly injuring by repeated biting, shaking, tearing, etc. From this original meaning the word has enlarged until now it means to tease, to trouble, to harass with importunity or with care or anxiety. In other words it is *undue* care, *needless* anxiety, *unnecessary* brooding, *fretting* thought.

What a wonderful picture the original source of the word suggests of the latter-day meaning. Worry takes our manhood, womanhood, our high ambitions, our laudable endeavors, our daily lives, *by the throat*, and strangles, chokes, bites, tears, shakes them, hanging on like a wolf, a weasel, or a bull-dog, sucking out our life-blood, draining our energies, our hopes, our aims, our noble desires, and leaving us torn, empty, shaken, useless, bloodless, hopeless, and despairing. It is the nightmare of life that rides us to discomfort, wretchedness, despair, and to that death-in-life that is no life at all. It is the vampire that sucks out the good of us and leaves us like the rind of a squeezed-out orange; it is the cooking-process that extracts and wastes all the nutritious juices of the meat and leaves nothing but the useless and tasteless fibre.

Worry is a worse thief than the burglar or highwayman. It goes beyond the train-wrecker or the vile wretch who used to lure sailing vessels upon a treacherous shore, in its relentless heartlessness. Once it begins to control it never releases its hold unless its victim wakes up to the sure ruin that awaits him and frees himself from its bondage by making a great, continuous, and successful fight.

It steals the joy of married life, of fatherhood and motherhood; it destroys social life, club life, business life, and religious life. It robs a man of friendships and makes his days long, gloomy periods, instead of rapidly-passing epochs of joy and happiness. It throws around its victim a chilling atmosphere as does the iceberg, or the snow bank; it exhales the mists and fogs of wretchedness and misunderstanding; it chills family happiness, checks friendly intercourse, and renders the business occupations of life curses instead of blessings.

Worry manifests itself in a variety of ways. It is protean in its versatility. It can be physical or mental. The hypochondriac conceives that everything is going to the "demnition bow-wows." Nothing can reassure him. He sees in every article of diet a hidden fiend of dyspepsia; in every drink a demon of torture. Every man he meets is a scoundrel, and every woman a leech. Children are growing worse daily, and society is "rotten." The Church is organized for the mere fattening of a raft of preachers and parsons who preach what they don't believe and never try to practice. Lawyers and judges are all dishonest swindlers caring nothing for honor and justice and seeking only their fees; physicians and surgeons are pitiless wretches who scare their patients in order to extort money from them; men in office are waiting, lurking, hunting for chances to graft, eager to steal from their constituents at every opportunity. He expects every thing, every animal, every man, every woman to get the best of him - and, as a rule, he is not disappointed. For we can nearly always be accommodated in life and get that for which we look.

We are told that all these imaginary ills come from physical causes. The hypochondrium is supposed to be affected, and as it is located under the "short ribs," the hypochondriac continuously suffers from that awful "sinking at the pit of the stomach" that makes him feel as if the bottom had dropped out of life itself. He can neither eat, digest his food, walk, sit, rest, work, take pleasure, exercise, or sleep. His body is the victim of innumerable ills. His tongue, his lips, his mouth are dry and parched, his throat full of slime and phlegm, his stomach painful, his bowels full of gas, and he regards himself as cursed of God - a walking recaptacle of woe. To physician, wife, husband, children, employer, employee, pastor, and friend alike the hypochondriac is a pest, a nuisance, a chill and almost a curse, and, poor creature, these facts do not take away or lessen our sympathy for him, for, though most of his ills are imaginary, he suffers more than do those who come in contact with him.

Then there is the neurasthenic - the mentally collapsed whose collapse invariably comes from too great tension or worry. I know several housewives who became neurasthenic by too great anxiety to keep their houses spotless. Not a speck of dust must be anywhere. The slightest appearance of inattention or carelessness in this matter was a great source of worry, and they worried lest the maid fail to do her duty.

I know another housewife who is so dainty and refined that, though her husband's income is strained almost to the breaking point, she must have everything in the house so dainty and fragile that no ordinary servant can be trusted to care for the furniture, wash the dishes, polish the floors, etc., and the result is she is almost a confirmed neurasthenic because, in the first place, she worries over her dainty things, and, secondly, exhausts herself in caring for these unnecessarily fragile household equipments.

Every neurasthenic is a confirmed worrier. He ever sits on the "stool of repentance," clothing himself in sackcloth and ashes for what he has done or not done. He cries aloud - by his acts - every five minutes or so: "We have done those things which we ought not to have done and have left undone those things which we ought to have done, and there is no health in us." Everything past is regretted, everything present is in doubt, and nothing but anxieties and uncertainties meet the future. If he holds a position of responsibility he asks his subordinates or associates to perform certain services and then "worries himself to death," watching to see that they "do it right," or afraid lest they forget to do it at all. He wakes up from a sound sleep in dread lest he forgot to lock the door, turn out the electric light in the hall, or put out the gas. He becomes the victim of uncertainty and indecision. He fears lest he decide wrongly, he worries that he hasn't yet decided, and yet having thoroughly argued a matter out and come to a reasonable conclusion, allows his worries to unsettle him and is forever questioning his decision and going back to revise and rerevise it. Whatever he does or doesn't do he regrets and wishes he had done the converse.

Husbands are worried about their wives; wives about their husbands; parents about their children; children about their parents. Farmers are worried over their crops; speculators over their gamblings; investors over their investments. Teachers are worried over their pupils, and pupils over their lessons, their grades, and their promotions. Statesmen (!) are worried over their constituents, and the latter are generally worried by their representatives. People who have schemes to further - legitimate or otherwise - are worried when they are retarded, and competitors are worried if they are not. Pastors are worried over their congregations, - occasionally about their salaries, very often about their large families, and now and again about their fitness for their holy office, - and there are few congregations that, at one time or another, are not worried *by*, as well as *about*, their pastors. The miner is worried when he sees his ledge "petering out," or finds the ore failing to assay its usual value. The editor is worried lest his reporters fail to bring in the news, and often worried when it is brought in to know whether it is accurate or not. The chemist worries over his experiments, and the inventor that certain things needful will persist in eluding him. The man who has to rent a house, worries when rent day approaches; and many who own houses worry at the same time. Some owners, indeed, worry because there is no rent day, they have no tenants, their houses are idle. Others worry because their tenants are not to their liking, are destructive, careless, or neglect the flowers and the lawn, or allow the children to batter the furniture, walk in hob nails over the hardwood floors, or scratch the paint off the walls. Men in high position worry lest their superiors are not as fully appreciative of their efforts as they should be, and they in turn worry their subordinates lest they forget that they are subordinate.

Mistresses worry about their maids, and maids about their mistresses. Some of the former worry because they have to go into their kitchens, others because they are not allowed to go. Some mistresses deliberately worry their servants, and others are worried because their servants insist upon doing the worrying. Many a wife is worried because of her husband's typewriter, and many a typewriter is worried because her employer has a wife. Some typewriters are worried because they are not made into wives, and many a one who is a wife wishes she were free again to become a typewriter.

Thousands of girls - many of them who ought yet to be wearing short dresses and playing with dolls - worry because they have no sweethearts, and equal thousands worry because they *do* have them. Many a lad worries because he has no "lassie," and many a one worries because he has. Yesterday I rode on a street car and saw a bit of by-play that fully illustrated this. On these particular cars there is a seat for two alongside the front by the motorman. On this car, chatting merrily with the handler of the lever, sat a black-eyed, pretty-faced Latin type of brunette. That *he* was happy was evidenced by his good-natured laugh and the huge smile that covered his face from ear to ear as he responded to her sallies. Just then a young Italian came on the car, directly to the front, and seemed nettled to see the young lady talking so freely with the motorman. He saluted her with a frown upon his face, but evidently with familiarity. The change in the girl's demeanor was instantaneous. Evidently she did not wish to offend the newcomer, nor did she wish to break with the motorman. All were ill at ease, distraught, vexed, worried. She tried to bring the newcomer into the conversation, which he refused. The motorman eyed him with hostility now and again, as he dared to neglect his duty, but smiled uneasily in the face of the girl when she addressed him with an attempt at freedom.

Bye and bye the youth took the empty seat by the side of the girl, and endeavored to draw her into conversation to the exclusion of the motorman. She responded, twisting her body and face towards him, so that her sweet and ingratiating smiles could not be seen by the motorman. Then, she reversed the process and gave a few fleeting smiles to the grim-looking motorman. It was as clear a case of

How happy could I be with either,
Were t'other dear charmer away,

as one could well see.

Just then the car came to a transfer point. The girl had a transfer and left, smiling sweetly, but separately, in turn, to the motorman and her young Italian friend. The latter watched her go. Then a new look came over his face, which I wondered at. It was soon explained. The transfer point was also a division point for this car. The motorman and conductor were changed, and the moment the new crew came, our motorman jumped from his own car, ran to the one the brunette had taken, and swung himself on, as it crossed at right angles over the track we were to take. Rising to his feet the youth watched the passing car, with keenest interest until it was out of sight, clearly revealing the jealousy, worry, and unrest he felt.

In another chapter I have dealt more fully with the subject of the worries of jealousy. They are demons of unrest and distress, destroying the very vitals with their incessant gnawing.

Too great emphasis cannot be placed upon the physical ills that come from worry. The body unconsciously reflects our mental states. A fretful and worrying mother should never be allowed to suckle her child, for she directly injures it by the poison secreted in her milk by the disturbances caused in her body by the worry of her mind. Among the many wonderfully good things said in his lifetime Henry Ward Beecher never said a wiser and truer thing than that "it is not the revolution which destroys the machinery, but the friction." Worry is the friction that shatters the machine. Work, to the healthy body and serene mind, is a joy, a blessing, a health-giving exercise, but to the worried is a burden, a curse and a destroyer.

Go where you will, when you will, how you will, and you will find most people worrying to a greater or lesser extent. Indeed so full has our Western world become of worry that a harsh and complaining note is far more prevalent than we are willing to believe, which is expressed in a rude motto to be found hung on many an office, bedroom, library, study, and laboratory wall which reads:

Life is one Damn

Those gifted with a sense of humor laugh at the motto; the very serious frown at it and reprobate its apparent profanity, those who see no humor in anything regard it with gloom, the careless with assumed indifference, but in the minds of all, more or less latent or sub-conscious, there is a recognition that there is "an awful lot of truth in it."

Hence it will be seen that worry is by no means confined to the poor. The well-to-do, the prosperous, and the rich, indeed, have far more to worry about than the poor, and for one victim who suffers keenly from worry among the poor, ten can be found among the rich who are its abject victims.

It is worry that paints the lines of care on foreheads and cheeks that should be smooth and beautiful; worry bows the shoulders, brings out scowls and frowns where smiles and sweet greetings should exist. Worry is the twister, the dwarfer, the poisoner, the murderer of joy, of peace, of work, of happiness; the strangler, the burglar of life; the phantom, the vampire, the ghost that scares, terrifies, fills with dread. Yet he is a liar and a scoundrel, a villain and a coward, who will turn and flee if fearlessly and courageously met and defied. Instead of pampering and petting him, humoring and conciliating him, meet him on his own ground. Defy him to do his worst. Flaunt him, laugh at his threats, sneer and scoff at his pretensions, bid him do his worst. Better be dead than under the dominion of such a tyrant. And, my word for it, as soon as you take that attitude, he will flee from you, nay, he will disappear as the mists fade away in the heat of the noonday sum.

Worry, however, is not only an effect. It is also a cause. Worry causes worry. It breeds more rapidly than do flies. The more one worries the more he learns to worry. Begin to worry over one thing and soon you are worrying about twenty. And the infernal curse is not content with breeding worries of its own kind. It is as if it were a parent gifted with the power of breeding a score, a hundred different kinds of progeny at one birth, each more hideous, repulsive, and fearful than the other. There is no palliation, temporization, or parleying possible with such a monster. Death is the only way to be released from him, and it is your death or his. His death is a duty God requires at your hands. Why, then, waste time? Start now and kill the foul fiend as quickly as you can.

CHAPTER II

OURS IS THE AGE OF WORRY

How insulting! What a ridiculous statement! How ignorant of our achievements! I can well imagine some of my readers saying when they see this chapter heading. *This*, an age of worry! Why this is the age of progress, of advancement, of uplift, of the onward march of a great and wonderful civilization.

Is it?

Certainly it is! See what we have done in electricity, look at the telephone, telegraph, wireless and now the wireless telephone. See our advancement in mechanics, - the automobile, the new locomotives, vessels, etc. See our conquest of the air - dirigibles, aeroplanes, hydroplanes and the like.

Yes! I see, and what of it? *We* have done, *our* advancement, *our* conquest, etc., etc. Yes! I see *we* have not lessened *our* arrogance, *our* empty-headed pride, *our* boasting. *We* - Why "*we*"?

What have you and I had to do with the new inventions in electricity or mechanics or the conquest of the air?

Not one single, solitary thing! The progress of the

world has been made through the efforts of a few solitary, exceptional, rare individuals, not by the combined efforts of us all. You and I are as common, unprogressive, uninventive, indifferent mediocrities as we - the common people - always were. We have not contributed one iota to all this progress, and I often question whether mud; of it comes to us more fraught with good than evil. We claim the results without engaging in the work. We use the 'phone and worry because Central doesn't get us our connections immediately, when we haven't the faintest conception of how the connection is gained, or why we are delayed. We ride on the fast train, but chafe and worry ourselves and everybody about us to a frazzle because we are stopped on a siding by a semaphore of a block station which we never have observed, and would not understand if we did. We reap but have not sowed, gather but have not strewed, and that is ever injurious and never beneficial. Our conceit is flattered and enlarged, our importance magnified, our "dignity" - God save the mark! - made more impressive, and as a result, we are more the target for the inconsequential worries of life. We worry if we are not flattered, if our importance is not recognized even by strangers, and our dignity not honored - in other words we worry that we are not *kow-towed* to, deferred to, respectfully greeted on every hand and made to feel that civilization, progress and advancement are materially furthered and enhanced by our mere existence.

Every individual with such an outlook on life is a prolific distributer of worry germs; he, she, is a pest and a nuisance, more disturbing to the real peace of the community than a victim of smallpox, and one who should be isolated in a pest-house. But, unfortunately, our myopic vision sees only the wealth, the luxury, the spending capacity of such an individual, and that ends it - we bow down and worship before the golden calf.

If I had the time in these pages to discuss the history of worry, I am assured I could show clearly to the student of history that worry is always the product of prosperity; that while a nation is hard at work at its making, and every citizen is engaged in arduous labor of one kind or another for the upbuilding of his own or the national power, worry is scarcely known. The builders of our American civilization were too busy conquering the wilderness of New England, the prairies of the Middle West, the savannahs and lush growths of the South, the arid deserts of the West to have much time for worry. Such men and women were gifted with energy, the power of initiative and executive ability, they were forceful, daring, courageous and active, and *in their very working* had neither time nor thought for worry.

But just as soon as a reasonable amount of success attended their efforts, and they had amassed wealth their children began and continued to worry. Not occupied with work that demands our unceasing energy, we find ourselves occupied with trifles, worrying over our health, our investments, our luxuries, our lap-dogs and our frivolous occupations. Imagine the old-time pioneers of the forest, plain, prairie and desert worrying about sitting in a draught, or taking cold if they got wet, or wondering whether they could eat what would be set before them at the next meal. They were out in the open, compelled to take whatever weather came to them, rain or shine, hot or cold, sleet or snow, and ready when the sunset hour came, to eat with relish and appetite sauce, the rude and plain victuals placed upon the table.

Compare the lives of that class of men with the later generation of "capitalists." I know one who used to live at Sherry's in New York. His apartments were as luxurious as those of a monarch; he was not happy, however, for worry rode him from morning to night. He absolutely spent an hour or more each day consulting the menu, or discussing with the steward what he could have to place upon his menu, and died long before his time, cursed with his wealth, its resultant idleness and the trifling worries that always come to such men. Had he been reduced to poverty, compelled to go out and work on a farm, eat oatmeal mush or starve for breakfast, bacon and greens for dinner, and cold pork and potatoes or starve for supper, he would be alive and happy to-day.

Take the fussy, nervous, irritable, worrying men and women of life, who poke their noses into other people's affairs, retail all the scandal, and hand on all the slander and gossip of empty and, therefore, evil minds. They are invariably well to do and without any work or responsibilities. They go gadding about restless and feverish because of the empty vacuity of their lives, a prey to worry because they have nothing else to do. If I were to put down and faithfully report the conversations I have with such people; the fool worries they are really distressed with; the labor, time and energy they spend on following chimeras, will o' the wisps, mirages that beckon to them and promise a little mental occupation, - and over which they cannot help but worry, one could scarcely believe it.

As Dr. Walton forcefully says in his admirable booklet:

The present, then, is the age, and our

contemporaries are the people, that bring into prominence the little worries, that cause the tempest in the teapot, that bring about the worship of the intangible, and the magnification of the unessential. If we had lived in another epoch we might have dreamt of the eternal happiness of saving our neck, but in this one we fret because our collar does not fit it, and because the button that holds the collar has rolled under the bureau.[A]

[Footnote A: *Calm Yourself.* By George Lincoln Walton, M.D., Houghton, Mifflin & Co., Boston, Mass.]

I am not so foolish as to imagine for one moment that I can correct the worrying tendency of the age, but I do want to be free from worry myself, to show others that it is unnecessary and needless, and also, that it is possible to live a life free from its demoralizing and altogether injurious influences.

CHAPTER III

NERVOUS PROSTRATION AND WORRY.

Nervous prostration is generally understood to mean weakness of the nerves. It invariably comes to those who have extra strong nerves, but who do not know how to use them properly, as well as those whose nervous system is naturally weak and easily disorganized. Nervous prostration is a disease of overwork, mainly mental overwork, and in ninety-nine cases out of a hundred, comes from worry. Worry is the most senseless and insane form of mental work. It is as if a bicycle-rider were so riding against time that, the moment after he got off his machine to sit down to a meal he sprang up again, and while eating were to work his arms and legs as if he were riding. It is the slave-driver that stands over the slave and compels him to continue his work, even though he is so exhausted that hands, arms and legs cease to obey, and he falls asleep at his task.

The folly, as well as the pain and distress of this cruel slave-driving is that we hold the whip over ourselves, have trained ourselves to do it, and have done it so long that now we seem unable to stop. In another chapter there is fully described (in Dorothy Canfield's vivid words) the squirrel-cage whirligig of modern society life. Modern business life is not much better.

Men compel themselves to the endless task of amassing money without knowing *why* they amass it. They make money, that they may enlarge their factories, to make more ploughs, to get more money, to enlarge their factories, to make more ploughs, to get more money, to enlarge more factories, to make more ploughs, and so on, *ad infinitum*. Where is the sense of it. Such conduct has well been termed money-madness. It is an obsession, a disease, a form of hypnotism, a mental malady.

The tendency of the age is to drive. We drive our own children to school; there they are driven for hours by one study after another; even when they come home they bring lessons with them - the lovers of study and over-conscientious because they want to do them, and the laggards because they must, if they are to keep up with their classes. If the parents of such children are not careful, they (the children) soon learn to worry; they are behind-hand with their lessons; they didn't get the highest mark yesterday; the class is going ahead of them, etc., etc., until mental collapse comes.

For worrying is the worst kind of mental overwork. As Dr. Edward Livingston Hunt, of Columbia University, New York, said in a paper read by him early in 1912, before the Public Health Education Committee of the Medical Society of the County of New York:

There is a form of overwork, exceedingly common and exceedingly disastrous - one which equally accompanies great intellectual labors and minor tasks. I allude to worry. When we medical men speak of the workings of the brain we make use of a term both expressive and characteristic. It is to cerebrate. To cerebrate means to think, to reason, and to reach conclusions; it means to concentrate and to work hard. To think, then, is to cerebrate. To worry is to cerebrate intensely.

Worry is overwork of the most disastrous kind; it means to drive the mental machinery at an unreasonable and dangerous rate. Worry gives the brain no rest, but rather keeps the delicate cells in constant and continuous action. Work is wear; worry is tear. Overwork, mental strain, and worry lead to a diminution of nerve force and to a prostration of the vital forces and causes a degeneracy of the blood vessels of the brain.

Exhaustion, another name for fatigue, may show itself either in the form of physical collapse, so that the patient lacks resistance, and, becoming anemic and run down, falls a prey to any and every little ailment, or in the form of mental collapse. An exhausted brain then gives way to depression, to fears, and to anxiety.

The vast majority of nervous breakdowns are avoidable; they are the result of our own excesses and of the disregard we show toward the ordinary laws of health and hygiene; they are the results of the tremendous demands which are made upon us by modern life; they are the result of the strenuous life.

From this analysis, made by an expert, it is evident that worry and nervous prostration are but two points on the same circle. Nervous prostration causes worry, and worry causes nervous prostration. Those who over-work their bodies and minds - who drive themselves either with the cares of business, the amassing of wealth, yielding to the demands of society, the cravings of ambition, or the pursuit of pleasure, are alike certain to suffer the results of mental overwork.

And here let me interject what to me has become a fundamental principle upon which invariably I rely. It will be recalled what I have said elsewhere of *selfish* and *unselfish* occupations. It is the selfish occupations that produce nerve-exhaustion. Those that are unselfish seldom result in the disturbance of the harmony or equilibrium of our nature - whether we regard it as physical, mental, or spiritual. This may seem to be a trancendental statement - perhaps it is. But I am confidently assured of its essential truth. That man or woman who is truly engaged in an unselfish work - a work that is for the good of others - has a right to look for, to expect and to receive from the great All Source of strength, power and serenity all that is needed to keep the body, mind and soul in harmony, consequently in perfect health and free from worry.

Hence the apparent paradox that, if you would care for yourself you must disregard yourself in your loving care for others.

One great reason why worry produces nervous prostration is that it induces insomnia.

Worry and sleeplessness are twin sisters. As one has well said: "Refreshing sleep and vexing thoughts are deadly foes." Health and happiness often disappear from those who fail to sleep, for sleep, indeed, is "tired Nature's sweet restorer," as Young in his *Night Thoughts* termed it. Shakspere never wrote anything truer when he said:

Sleep that knits up the ravell'd sleave of care,
The death of each day's life, sore labor's bath,
Balm of hurt minds, great Nature's second course,
Chief nourisher of life's feast.

Or, where he spoke of it as

Sleep that sometimes shuts up sorrow's eye,
Steals me awhile from mine own company.

Even the Bible makes sleep one of the special blessings of God, for we are told that "He giveth His beloved sleep." The sacred book contains many references to sleeplessness and its causes.

Undoubtedly most potent among these causes is worry. The worrier retires to his bed at the usual hour, but his brain is busy - it is working overtime. What is it doing? Is it thinking over things that are to be done, and planning for the future? If so, there is a legitimate excuse, for as soon as the plan is laid, rest will come, and he will sleep. Is he thinking over the mistakes of the past and sensibly and wisely taking counsel from them? If so, he will speedily come to a decision, and then sleep will bring grateful oblivion. Is he thinking joyful thoughts? These will bring a natural feeling of harmony with all things, and that is conducive to speedy sleep? Is he thinking of how he may help others? That is equally soothing to nerves, brain and body, and brings the refreshment of forgetfulness.

But no! the worrier has another method. He thinks the same thoughts over and over again, without the slightest attempt to get anywhere. He has thrashed them out before, so often that he can tell exactly what each thought will lead to. His ideas go around in a circle like the horse tied to the wheel. He is on a treadmill ever ascending, tramping, up, up, up and up, and still up, but the wheel falls down each time as far as he steps up, and after hours and hours of unceasing, wracking, distressful mental labor, he has done absolutely nothing, has not progressed one inch, is still in the clutch of the same vicious treadmill. Brain weary, nerve weary, is there any wonder that he rolls and tosses, throws over his pillow, kicks off the clothes, groans, almost cries aloud in his agony of longing for rest. Poor victim of worry and sleepless-ness, how I long to help you get rid of your evil habit and save others from falling into it. For both worry and sleeplessness are habits, easily gained, and once gained very hard to get rid of, yet both unnecessary, needless, and foolish. The worry that produces sleeplessness is merciless; so merciless and relentless that no fierce torture of a Black-hander can be described that is worse in its long continuing and evil results. Lives are wrecked, brains shattered, happiness destroyed by this monstrous evil, and many a man and woman fastens it upon himself, herself, through indulging in anxious thought, or by yielding to that equal devil-dragon of self-pity.

David the psalmist graphically tells of his own case:

I am weary with my groaning;
Every night make I my bed to swim;
I water my couch with my tears,
Mine eye wasteth away because of grief.
Ps. VI. 6:7.

At another time he cries

My God, my God, why hast thou forsaken me?

Why art thou so far from helping me, and from the words of my groaning?

Oh my God, I cry in the day time, but thou answereth not;

And in the night season, I am not silent. *Ps. XXII.* 1:2.

Yet God heard him not until his groaning and self-pity were cast aside, until he rested in God, trusted in Him. Then came rest, as he graphically expresses it:

I laid me down and slept;
I awaked; for Jehovah sustaineth me. *Ps. III. 5.*

In peace will I both lay me down and sleep:
For thou, Jehovah, alone maketh me dwell in safety.
Ps. IV. 8.

I will bless Jehovah, who hath given me counsel;
Yea, my heart instructeth me in the night seasons.
Ps. XVI. 7.

See the result of this confidence in God.

I have set Jehovah always before me:
Because he is at my right hand, I shall not be moved.

Therefore my heart is glad, and my glory rejoiceth:
My flesh also shall dwell in safety. *Ps. XVI. 8:9.*

And where the heart is glad, and one rejoiceth in the sense of peace and safety, sweet sleep lays its soothing hand upon the work-worn brain and body, tired with the labors of the day, and brings rest, repose, recuperation.

CHAPTER IV

HOLY WRIT, THE SAGES, AND WORRY

Our civilization is called a *Christian* civilization. We are the *Christian* nations. Yet, as I have shown in Chapters I and II, ours is the worrying civilization. That worry is dishonoring to our civilization, and especially to our professions as Christians is self-evident. Let us then look briefly in the book we call our Holy Bible, our Guide of Life, our Director to Salvation, and see what the sacred writers have to say upon this subject. If they commend it, we may assume that it will be safe to worry. If they rebuke or reprobate it we may be equally assured that we have no right to indulge in it.

St. Paul seemed to have a very clear idea of worry when he said:

> Be careful - [full of care] - for nothing, but in everything by prayer and supplication, with thanksgiving, make your requests known unto God. *Philippians* 4:6.

How inclusive this is - full of care, anxiety, fretfulness, worry about *nothing*, but in *everything* presenting your case to God. And then comes the promise:

And the peace of God which passeth all understanding shall keep your hearts and minds in Christ Jesus. *Phil.* IV. 7.

How clear, definite, full and satisfactory. What room for worry is there in a heart full of the peace of God, which passeth all understanding? And oh, how much to be desired is such an experience.

Browning, in his *Abt Vogler*, sings practically the same sweet song where he says:

> Sorrow is hard to bear, and doubt is slow to clear,
> Each sufferer says his says, his scheme of the weal and woe:
> But God has a few of us whom He whispers in the ear;
> The rest may reason and welcome; 'tis we musicians know.

If God whispers in the ear of the sufferer, the doubter, the distressed, the worried, the peace must come; and if peace come, it matters not what others' reasoning may bring to them, the knowledge that God has whispered is enough; it brings satisfaction, content, serenity, peace. The opposite of worry is rest, faith, trust, peace. How full the Bible is of promises of rest to those who know and love God and his ways of right-doing. Mendlessohn took the incitement of the psalmist (Psalm 37:7), "Rest in the Lord, and wait patiently for him," and made of it one of the tenderest, sweetest songs of all time. Full of yearning over the worried, the distressed, the music itself seems to brood in sympathetic and soothing power, as a mother croons to her fretful child: "Why fret, why worry, - No, no! rest, rest my little one, in the love of the all-Father," and many a weary, fretful, worried heart has found rest and peace while listening to this sweet and beautiful song.

There is still another passage in holy writ that the perpetual worrier should read and ponder. It is the prophet Isaiah's assurance that God says to His children: "As one whom his mother comforteth, so will I comfort you."

Who has not seen a fretful, sick child taken up by a loving mother, yield to her soothing influence in a few minutes and drop off into restful, healthful, restoring sleep. What a wonderful and forceful figure of speech, illustrative of a never-ceasing fact that the Spirit of all good, the supreme Force of Love and Power in the universe is looking, watching, without slumber or sleep, untiring, unfailing, ever ready to give soothing comfort as does the mother, to those who fret and worry.

Then, when cause for worry seems to be ever present, why not call upon this Loving Maternal Soothing Power? Why not rest in His arms, and thus find peace, poise and serenity?

How much worry comes from fear as to the future. Men become hoarders, savers, misers, or work themselves beyond healthful endurance, or shut out the daily joys of existence in their business absorption, because they dread poverty in their old age. "Wise provision" becomes a driving monster, worrying them into a restless, fretful energy that must be accumulating all the time.

Two thousand years ago this trait of human nature was so strongly manifested that Christ felt called upon to restrain and rebuke it. What a wonderful sermon He preached. It is worth while repeating it here, and wise would that man, that woman be, who is worried about to-morrow, were he, she, to read it daily. I give it in the revised version:

I say unto you, Be not anxious for your life, what ye shall eat, or what ye shall drink; nor yet for your body, what ye shall put on. Is not the life more than the food, and the body than the raiment? Behold the birds of the heaven, that they sow not, neither do they reap, nor gather into barns; and your Heavenly Father feedeth them. Are not ye of much more value than they? And which of you by being anxious can add one cubit unto his stature? And why are ye anxious concerning raiment? Consider the lilies of the field, how they grow; they toil not, neither do they spin; yet I say unto you, that even Solomon in all his glory was not arrayed like one of these. But if God doth so clothe the grass of the field, which to-day is, and to-morrow is cast into the oven, shall he not much more clothe you, O ye of little faith? Be not therefore anxious, saying, What shall we eat? or, What shall we drink? or, Wherewithal shall we be clothed? For after all these things do the Gentiles seek; for your heavenly Father knoweth that ye have need of all these things. But seek ye first his kingdom, and his righteousness; and all these things shall be added unto you. Be not therefore anxious for the morrow: for the morrow will be anxious for itself. Sufficient unto the day is the evil thereof. *Matthew*, 6:25-34.

Here is the wisest philosophy. Anxiety is suicide, peace is life; worry destroys, serenity upbuilds. As you want to live, to grow, possess your souls in peace and

George Wharton James

serenity. Work, aye, work mightily, powerfully, daily, but work for the joy of it, not because worry drives you to it. Work persistently, consistently and worthily, because no man can live - or ought to live - without it, but do not let work be your slave driver, your relentless master, urging you on to drudgery, bondage to your counter, ledger or factory, until you drop exhausted and lifeless. Work for the real joy of it, and then, filled with the blessed trust in God the all-Father expressed as above by Christ, throw your cares to the winds, bid your worries depart, and accept what comes with serenity, peace and thankfulness.

Many proverbs have been written about worry, which it may be well to recall. Certainly it can do no harm to those who worry to see how their mental habit has been regarded, and is still regarded, by the concentrated wisdom of the ages.

An old proverb says: "It is not work, but worry, that kills." How true this is. Congenial work is a health-bringer, a necessity for a normal life, a joy; it keeps the body in order, promotes digestion, induces the sleep of perfect restoration and is one of man's greatest blessings. But worry brings dis-ease (want of ease), discomfort, wretchedness, promotes evil secretions which upset the normal workings of the body, and is a constant banisher and disturber of sleep.

Still another proverb says: "Worry killed the cat." Many people read this and fail to see its profound significance. It must be remembered that in "the good old days," when this proverb was most rife, the superstitious held that a cat had *nine lives*. Now, surely, the deep meaning of the proverb is made apparent. Though the cat were possessed of nine lives, worry would surely kill them all - either one by one, by its horrid and determined persistence; or all at once, by the concentrated virulence of its power.

There are many proverbs to the effect that "When worry comes in, wit flies out," and these are all true. Worry unsettles the mind, unbalances the judgment, induces fever of the intellect, which renders calm, cool weighing of matters impossible. No man of great achievements ever worried during his period of greatness. Had he done so his greatness could never have been achieved. Imagine a general trying to solve the vexing problems of a great combat which is going against him, with his mind beset by numberless worries. He must concentrate *all his energies* upon the one thing. If worry occupies his attention, wit, sense, judgment, discretion, wisdom are crowded out, have no place.

All the pictures given to us of Grant show him the most imperturbable at the most trying times. When the fortunes of war seemed most against him he was the most cheerful, the least disturbed. He had learned the danger of worry, and compelled it to flee from him, that calm judgment and clear-headed decisions might be his.

If, therefore, these great ones of earth found it essential to their well-being to banish worry, how much more is it necessary that we of the ordinary mass of mankind, of the commoner herd, apply ourselves to the gaining of the same kind of wisdom.

An old countrywoman once said in my hearing: "Worry, and you hug a hornet's nest." How suggestive both of the stinging that was sure to come and the folly, the absurdity, the cruelty to oneself of the act.

The great Scotch philosopher, Blair, said: "Worry (or anxiety) is the poison of human life," and how true it is. How biting, how corroding, how destructive to life some poisons are, working speedily, suddenly, awfully. Others there are that have a cumulative effect, until life itself cannot bear the strain, and it goes out. Recently I was at a home where a son was so worried over conditions that he felt ought not to exist between his parents, that he totally collapsed, mentally, and for a time was in danger of losing his reason. The folly of his attitude is apparent to everyone but himself, though he now seeks in the absorbing occupation of teaching, to free himself from the poison of worry that was speedily destroying his reason.

Henry Labouchere, the sage who for so many years has edited the London *Truth*, once wrote a couplet, that is as true as anything he ever wrote:

They who live in a worry,
Invite death in a hurry.

I want to be ready for death when it comes, but as yet I am not extending an invitation to the gentleman with the scythe. Are you, my worrying reader, anxious to be mowed down before your time? Quit your worrying, and don't urge the Master Reaper to harvest you in until He is sure you are ready.

Another sage once said: "To worry about to-morrow is to be unhappy to-day," and the same thought is put into: "Never howl till you are hit," and the popular proverb attributed erroneously to Lincoln for it was long in use before Lincoln's time: "Do not cross the stream until you get to it." Christ put the same thought into his Sermon on the Mount, when He said: "Sufficient unto the day is the evil thereof." How utterly foolish and wrong it is to spoil to-day by fretting and worrying over the possible evils of to-morrow. Many a man in business has ruined himself by allowing worries about to-morrow to prevent him from doing the needful work of to-day. The rancher who sits down and worries because he fears it will not rain to-morrow, or it will rain, fails to do the work of to-day ready for whatever the morrow may bring forth. The wise Roman, Seneca, expressed the same thing in other words when he wrote: "He grieves more than is necessary who grieves before it is necessary," and our own Lowell had a similar thought in mind which he expressed as follows: "The misfortunes hardest to bear are those which never come." Even the Chinese saw the folly of worrying over events that have not yet transpired, for they have a saying: "To what purpose should a person throw himself into the water before the boat is cast away (wrecked)."

All these proverbs, therefore, show that the wisdom of the ages is against worrying over things that have not yet transpired. Let to-morrow take care of itself. Live to-day. As Cardinal Newman's wonderful hymn expresses it:

> I do not ask to see the distant scene,
> One step enough for me.

Furthermore, the evil we dread for to-morrow may never come. Every man's experience demonstrates this. The bill for which he has not money in the bank is met by the unexpected payment of an account overdue, or not yet due. Hence if fears come of the morrow, if we are tempted to worry about a grief that seems to be approaching, let us resolutely cast the temptation aside, and by a full occupation of mind and body in the work of the "now," engage ourselves beyond the possibility of hearing the voice of the tempter.

When one considers the words that are regarded as synonymous with "worry," or that are related to it, he sees what cruelties lurk in the facts behind the words. To grieve, fret, pine, mourn, bleed, chafe, yearn, droop, sink, give way to despair, all belong to the category of worry.

Phrases like "to sit on thorns," "to be on pins and needles," "to drain the cup of misery to the dregs," show with graphic power the folly and curse of worry. Why should one sit on thorns, or on pins and needles? If one does so accidentally he arises in a hurry, yet in worrying, one seems deliberately, with intent, to sit down upon prickles in order to compel himself to discomfort, distress, and pain. Is there any wisdom, when one has the cup of misery at his lips, in deliberately keeping it there, and persistently drinking it to the "very dregs"? One unconsciously feels like shouting to the drinker: "Put it down, you fool!" and if the harsh command be not instantly obeyed, rushing up and dashing it out of the drinker's hand.

Take a few more words and look at them, and see how closely they are related to worry, - to be displeased, fretted, annoyed, incommoded, discomposed, troubled, disquieted, crossed, teased, fretted, irked, vexed, grieved, afflicted, distressed, plagued, bothered, pestered, bored, harassed, perplexed, haunted. These things worry does to those who yield themselves to its noxious power.

Worry deliberately pains, wounds, hurts, pinches, tweaks, grates upon, galls, chafes, gnaws, pricks, lancinates, lacerates, pierces, cuts, gravels, corrodes, mortifies, shocks, horrifies, twinges and gripes its victims.

It smites, beats, punishes, wrings, harrows, torments, tortures, racks, scarifies, crucifies, convulses, agonizes, irritates, provokes, stings, nettles, maltreats, bites, snaps at, assails, badgers, harries, persecutes, those who give it shelter.

Is it not apparent, then, that the only course open for a sensible man or woman is to

QUIT WORRYING.

CHAPTER V

THE NEEDLESSNESS AND
USELESSNESS OF WORRY

Of all the mental occupations fallen into, invented, or discovered by man, the most needless, futile, and useless of all is the occupation of worry. We have heard it said often, when one was speaking of another's work, or something he had done: "He ought to be in a better business." So, *in every case*, can it be said of the worrier: He's in a bad business; a business that ought not to exist, one without a single redeeming feature. If for no other reason the fact implied by the title of this chapter ought to be sufficient to condemn it. Worry is needless, useless, futile, of none effect. Why push a heavy rock up a mountain side merely to have it roll down again? Yet one might find good in the physical development that came from this needless uphill work. And he might laugh, and sing, and be cheery while he was doing it. But in the case of the worrier he not only pushes the rock up the hill, but he is beset with the dread that, every moment, it is going to roll back and kill him, and he thinks of nothing but the fear, and the strain, and the distress.

When one calmly considers, it is almost too ridiculous to write seriously about the needlessness and useless-ness of worry; its futility is so self-evident to an intelligent mind. Yet, because so many otherwise intelligent and good people are cursed by it, it seems necessary to show its utter uselessness. These say: "I would stop worrying if I could; but I can't help it; I worry in spite of myself!"

Don't you believe it! You doubtless think your statement is true, but it is nothing of the kind. Worry could find no place in your mind if it was full to overflowing with something really useful and beneficial. It is a proof either that your mind bosses you, - in other words, that you cannot direct it to think upon something worth while, that it is absolutely untrained, undisciplined, uncontrolled, - or that it is so empty, it takes to worry as a refuge against its own vacuity. The fact of worry implies either that the worrier has no control over his mind, or has an empty mind.

Now no intelligent person will, for one moment, confess to such weakness of mind that he has no control over it. An unoccupied mind can always be occupied if one so wills. No human being is so constituted that nothing appeals to him or interests him, so every mind can be awakened and filled with contemplation of good things - things that will help, benefit and bless, if he so desires.

In the Foreword I have referred to my own experience. Many who knew some of the facts and saw the change that came over my life, have asked me *how* I succeeded in eliminating worry. I refused to allow my mind to dwell upon harassing topics or events in my life. If I awoke during the night, I turned on the light and picked up a book and forced my thought into another channel. If the objectionable thoughts obtruded during the day I did one of many things, as, for instance, turned to my work with a frenzy of absorption; picked up my hat and went for a walk; called upon friends; went to a concert; or a vaudeville show; took in a lecture; stood and watched the crowds; visited the railway stations - anything, everything, but dwell upon the subjects that were tabooed.

Here was a simple and practical remedy, and I found it worked well. But I can now see that there was a much better way. Where good is substituted for evil one has "the perfect way," and the Apostle Paul revealed himself a wise man of practical affairs, when he urged his readers to "think on the things" that are lovely, pure, just, and of good report. In my case I merely sought to prevent mental vacuity so that the seven devils of worry could not rush into, and take possession of, my empty mind; but I was indifferent, somewhat, to the kind of thought or mental occupation that was to keep out the thoughts of worry. A Nick Carter detective story was as good as a Browning poem, and sometimes better; a cheap and absurd show than an uplifting lecture or concert. How much better it would have been could I have had my mind so thoroughly under control - and this control can surely be gained by any and every man, woman, and child that lives, - that, when worrying thoughts obtruded, I could have said immediately and with authoritative power: I will to think on this thing, or that, or the other. The result would have been an immediate and perfect cessation of the worry that disturbed, fretted, and destroyed, for the mind would have become engaged with something that was beneficial and helpful. And remember this: God is good, and it is His pleasure to help those who are seeking to help themselves. Or to put it in a way that even our agnostic friends can receive, Nature is on the side of the man or woman who is seeking to live naturally, that is, rightly. Hence, substitute good thoughts for the worrying thoughts and the latter will fade away as do the mist and fog before the morning sun.

Here, then, I had clearly demonstrated for myself the needlessness of worry: *I could prevent it if I would.* And my readers cannot too soon gain this positive assurance. They *can*, if they *will*. It is simply a question of wanting to be free earnestly enough to work for freedom. Is freedom from worry worth while; is it worth struggling for? To me, it is one of the great blessings of life that worry is largely, if not entirely, eliminated. I would not go back to the old worrying days for all the wealth of Morgan, Rockefeller, and Carnegie combined.

As for the uselessness of worry; who is there, that has studied the action of worry, that ever found any of the problems it was concerned over improved by all the hours of worry devoted to it. Worry never solved a problem yet; worry muddies the water still further instead of clearing it; worry adds to the tangle instead of releasing it; worry beclouds the mind, prevents sane judgment, confuses the reason, and leads one to decisions that never ought to be made, and so to an uncertainty, as vexatious and irritating as is the original problem to be solved. If the worry pointed a way out of the difficulty I would extol worry and regard it as a bitter draught of medicine, to be swallowed in a hurry, but producing a beneficial result. But it never does anything to help; it invariably hinders; it sets one chasing shadows, produces *ignes fatui* before the eyes, and ultimately leads one into the bog.

Elsewhere I have referred to the Indians' attitude of

mind. If a matter can be changed, change it; if not grin and bear it without complaint. Here is practical wisdom. But to worry over a thing that can be changed, instead of changing it, is the height of folly, and if a matter cannot be changed why worry over it? How utterly useless is the worry. Then, too, worry is the parent of nagging. Nagging is worry put into words, - the verbal expression of worry about or towards individuals. The mother wishes her son would do differently. Can the boy's actions be changed? Then go to work to change them - not to worry over them. If they cannot be changed, why nag him, why irritate him, why make a bad matter worse? Nagging, like worry, never once did one iota of good; it has caused infinite harm, as it sets up an irritation between those whose love might overcome the difficulty if it were let alone. Nagging is the constant irritation of a wound, the rubbing of a sore, the salting an abraded place, the giving a hungry man a tract, religious advice or a bible, when all he craves is food.

Ah, mother! many a boy has run away from home because your worry led you to nag him; many a girl to-day is on the streets because father or mother nagged her; many a husband has "gone on a tear" because he could not face his wife's "worry put into words," even though no one would attempt to deny that boy, girl and husband alike were wrong *in every particular*, and the "nagger" in the right, save in the one thing of worry and its consequent nagging.

In watching the lives of men and women I have been astonished, again and again, that the fruitlessness of their worry did not demonstrate its uselessness to them. No good ever comes from it. Everybody who has any perception sees this, agrees to it, confesses it. Then why still persist in it? Yet they do, and at the same time expect to be regarded as intelligent, sane, normal human beings, many of whom claim, as members of churches, peculiar and close kinship with God, forgetful of the fact that every moment spent in worry is dishonoring to God.

How much needless anxiety, care, and absolute torture some women suffer in an insane desire to keep their homes spotlessly clean. The house must be without a speck of dirt anywhere; the kitchen must be as spotless as the parlor; the sink must be so immaculate that you could eat from it, if necessary; the children must always be in their best bibs and tuckers and appear as Little Lord Fauntleroys; and no one, at any time, or any circumstance, must ever appear to be dirty, except the scavenger who comes to remove the accumulated debris of the kitchen, and the man who occasionally assists the gardener.

These people forget that all dirt and dust is not of greater value than spotless cleanliness. Let us look calmly at the problem for a few minutes. Here is a housewife who cannot afford help to keep her house as spotless as her instincts and her training desire. It is simply impossible for her, personally, to go over the house daily with rag, duster and dustpan. If she attempts it, as she does sometimes - she overworks, and a breakdown is the result. What, then, is the sensible, the reasonable, the only thing she should do? Sit down and "worry" over her "untidy house"; lament that "the stairs have not been swept since day before yesterday; that the parlor was not dusted this morning; the music-room looks simply awful," and cry that "if Mrs. Brown were to come in and see my wretchedly untidy house, I'm sure I should die of shame!" Would this help matters? Would one speck of dirt be removed as the result of the worry, the wailing, and the tears? Not a speck. Every particle would remain just as before.

Yet other things would not be as they were before. No woman could feel as I have suggested this "worriting creature" felt, without gendering irritation in husband, children and friends. Is any house that was ever built worth the alienation of dear ones? What is the dust, dirt, disorder, of a really untidy house - I am supposing an extraordinary case - compared with the irritation caused by a worrying housewife?

Furthermore: such a woman is almost sure to break down her own health and become an irritable neuras- thenic or hypochondriac, and thus add to the burdens of those she loves.

There are women who, instead of following this course, make themselves wretched - and everyone else around them - by the worry of contrasting their lot with that of some one more fortunately situated than they. _She_ has a husband who earns more money than does hers; such an one has a larger allowance and can afford more help - the worry, however, is the same, little matter what form it takes, and worry is the destructive thing.

What, then, shall a woman do, who has to face the fact that she cannot gratify her desire to keep her house immaculate, either because she has not the strength to do it, or the money to hire it done. The old proverb will help her: "What can't be cured must be endured." There is wonderful help in the calm, full, direct recognition of unpleasant facts. Look them squarely in the face. Don't dodge them, don't deny them. Know them, understand them, then defy them to destroy your happiness. If you can't dust your house daily, dust it thrice a week, or twice, or once, and determine that you will be happy in spite of the dust. The real comfort of the house need not thereby be impaired, as there is a vast difference between your scrupulous cleanliness and careless untidiness. Things may be in order even though the floor has a little extra dust on, or the furniture has not been dusted for four days.

"But," you say, "I am far less disturbed by the over work than I am by the discomfort that comes from the dust." Then all I can say is that you are wrongly balanced, according to my notion of things. Your health should be of far more value to you than your ideas of house tidiness, but you have reversed the importance of the two. Teach yourself the relative value of things. A hundred dollar bill is of greater value than one for five dollars, and the life of your baby more important than the value of the hundred dollar bill. Put first things first, and secondly, and tertiary, and quarternary things in their relative positions. Your health and self-poise should come first, the comfort and happiness of husband and family next, the more or less spotlessness and tidiness of the house afterwards. Then, if you cannot have your house as tidy as you wish, resolutely resolve that you will not be disturbed. You will control your own life and not allow a dusty room - be it never so dusty - to destroy your comfort and peace of mind, and that of your loved ones.

When a woman of this worrying type has children she soon learns that she must choose between the health and happiness of her children and the gratification of her own passionate desire for spotless cleanliness. This gratification, if permanently indulged in, soon becomes a disease, for surely only a diseased mind can value the spotlessness of a house more than the health, comfort, and happiness of children. Yet many women do - more's the pity. Such poor creatures should learn that there is a dirtiness that is far worse than dirt in a house - a dirtiness, a muddiness of mind, a cluttering of thought, a making of the mind a harboring place for wrong thoughts. Not wrong in the sense of immoral or wicked, as these words are generally used, but wrong in this sense, viz., that reason shows the folly, the inutility, the impracticability of attempting to bring up sane, healthy, happy, normal children in a household controlled by the idea that spotless cleanliness is the matter of prime importance to be observed. The discomfort of children, husband, mother herself are nothing as compared with keeping the house in perfect order. Any woman so obsessed should be sent for a short time to an insane asylum, for she certainly has so reversed the proper order of values as to be so far insane. She has "cluttered up" her mind with a wrong idea, an idea which dirties, muddies, soils her mind far worse than dust soils her house.

Reader, keep your mind free from such dirt - for dirt is but "matter in the wrong place." Far better have dust, dirt, in your house, dirt on your child's hands, face, and clothes, than on your own mind to give you worry, discomfort and disease.

CHAPTER VI

THE SELFISHNESS OF WORRY

If worry merely affected the one who worries it might be easier, in many cases, to view worry with equanimity and calmness. But, unfortunately, in the disagreeable features of life, far more than the agreeable, the aphorism of the apostolic writer, "No man liveth unto himself," seems to be more than ordinarily true. It is one proof of the selfishness of the "worrier" - whether consciously or unconsciously I do not say - that he never keeps his worry to himself. He must always "out with it." The nervous mother worrying about her baby shows it even to the unconscious child at her breast. When the child is older she still shows it, until the little one knows as well as it knows when the sun is shining that "mother is worrying again." The worrying wife does not keep her worry to herself; she pours it out to, or upon, her husband. The worrying husband is just the same. If it is the wife that causes him to worry - or to think so - he pours out his worry in turbulent words, thus adding fuel to a fire already too hot for comfort.

It is one of the chief characteristics of worry that it is seldom confined to the breast of its victim. It loses its power, too often, when shut up. It must find expression in looks, in tone of voice, in sulkiness, in dumps, in nagging or in a voicing of its woes.

It is in this voicing of itself that worry demonstrates its inherent selfishness. If father, mother, wife, friends, neighbors, *anybody* can give help, pleasure, joy, instruction, profit, their voices are always heard with delight. If they have reasonable cautions to give to those they love, who seem to them to be thoughtless, regardless of danger which they see or fear, or even foolhardy, let them speak out bravely, courageously, lovingly, and they will generally be listened to. But to have them voice their fretful, painful, distressing worries no one is benefitted, and both speaker and the one spoken to are positively harmed. For an unnecessary fear voiced is strengthened; it is made more real. If one did not feel it before, it is now planted in his mind to his serious detriment, and once there, it begins to breed as disease germs are said to breed, by millions, and one moment of worry weds another moment, and the next moment a family of worries is born that surround, hamper and bewilder. Is this kindly, is it helpful, is it loving, is it unselfish?

The questions answer themselves. The planting of worry in the mind of another is heartless, cruel, unkind and selfish.

Another question naturally arises: If this course of action is selfish, and the worrier really desires to be unselfish, how can he control his worry, at least so as not to communicate it to another? The answer also is clear.

Let him put a guard upon his lips, a watch upon his actions. Let him say to himself: Though I do not, for my own sake, care to control the needless worries of my life, I must not, I dare not curse other lives with them. Hence I must at least keep them to myself - I must not voice them, I must not display them in face, eyes or tone.

Then there is the mother who worries over her child's clothing. She is never ceasing in her cautions. It is "don't, don't, don't," from morning to night, and whether this seems "nagging" to her or not, there would be a unanimous vote on the subject were the child consulted as to his feelings. Of course the boy, the girl, must be taught to take care of his, her, clothes, but this is never done by nagging. A far better plan would be to fit a punishment which really belongs to the evil or careless habit of the child. For instance, if a boy will persist in throwing his hat anywhere, instead of hanging it up, let the parent give him *one* caution, not in a threatening or angry way, but in just as matter of fact a fashion as if she were telling him of some news: "John, the next time you fail to hang your hat in its proper place I shall lock it up for three days!"

Then, if John fails, take the hat and lock it up, and *let it stay locked-up*, though the heavens fall. The same with a child's playthings, tennis racquets, base-balls, bats, etc. As a rule one application of the rule cures. This is immeasurably more sensible than nagging, for it produces the required result almost instantly, and there is little irritation to either person concerned, while nagging is never effective, and irritates both all the time.

Other parents worry considerably over their children getting in the dirt.

In an article which recently appeared in *Good*

Housekeeping Dr. Woods Hutchinson says some sensible things on "Children as Cabbages." He starts out by saying: "It is well to remember that not all dirt is dirty. While some kinds of dirt are exceedingly dangerous, others are absolutely necessary to life."

If your children get into the dirty and dangerous dirt, spend your energies in getting them into the other kind of dirt, rather than in nagging. Fall into the habit of doing the wise, the rational, the sane thing, because it produces results, rather than the foolish, irrational, insane thing which never produces a result save anger, irritation, and oftentimes, alienation.

In a little book written by J.J. Bell, entitled *Wee MacGregor*, there is a worrying mother. Fortunately she is sweet-spirited with it all, or it would have been unbearable.

She and her husband John, and the baby, wee Jeannie, with Macgregor were going out to dinner at "Aunt Purdie's," who was "rale genteel an' awfu' easy offendit." The anxious mother was counselling her young son regarding his behavior at the table of that excellent lady:

> 'An' mind, Macgreegor, ye're no' to be askin' fur jeely till ye've ett twa bits o' breed-an'-butter. It's no' mainners; an' yer Aunt Purdie's rale partecclar. An' yer no' to dicht yer mooth wi' yer cuff - mind that. Ye're to tak' yer hanky an' let on ye're jist gi'ein' yer nib a bit wipe. An' ye're no' to scale yer tea nor sup the sugar if ony's left in yer cup when ye're dune drinkin'. An' if ye drap yer piece on the floor ye're no' to gang efter it; ye're jist to let on ye've ett it. An' ye're no' -

'Deed, Lizzie,' interposed her husband, 'ye're the yin to think aboot things.'

'Weel, John, if I dinna tell Macgreegor hoo to behave hissel', he'll affront me,' etc., etc., etc.

Who has not thus seen the anxious mother? And who ever saw her worrying and anxiety do much if any good? Train your child by all means in your own home, but let up when you are going out, for your worry worries him, makes him self-conscious, brings about the very disasters you wish to avoid, and at the same time destroys his, your, and everyone's else, pleasure who observes, feels, or hears the expressions of worry.

CHAPTER VII

CAUSES OF WORRY

Worry is as multiform and as diverse as are the people who worry. Indeed worriers are the most ingenious persons in the world. When every possible source of worry seems to be removed, they proceed immediately to invent some new cause which an ordinary healthful mind could never have conceived.

The causes of worry are innumerable. They represent the sum total of the errors, faults, missteps, unholy aims, ambitions, foibles, weaknesses and crimes of men. Every error, mistake, weakness, crime, etc., is a source of worry - a cause of worry. Worry is connected only with the weak, the human, the evil side of human nature. It has no place whatever in association with goodness, purity, holiness, faith, courage and trust in God. When good men and women worry, in so far as they worry they are not good. Their worry is a sign of weakness, of lack of trust in God, of unbelief, of unfaithfulness. The man who knows God and his relationship to man; who knows his own spiritual nature and his relationship to God *never worries*. There is no possible place in such a man's life for worry.

Hence it will be seen that I believe worry to be evil, and nothing but evil, and, therefore, without one reclaiming or redeeming feature, for it can be productive of nothing but evil.

If you really desire to know the sources of your worry *study each worry as it comes up.* Analyse it, dissect it, weigh it, examine it from every standpoint, judge it by the one test that everything in life must, and ought to submit to, viz.: its usefulness. What use is it to you? How necessary to your existence? How helpful is it in solving the problems that confront you; how far does it aid you in their solution, wherein does it remove the obstacles before your pathway. Find out how much it strengthens, invigorates, inspires you. Ask yourself how much it encourages, enheartens, emboldens you. Put down on paper every slightest item of good, or help, or inspiration it is to you, and on the other hand, the harm, the discouragement, the evil, the fears it brings to you, and then strike a balance.

I can tell you beforehand that after ten years' study - if so long were necessary - you will fail to find one good thing in favor of worry, and that every item you will enumerate will be against it. Hence, why worry? Quit it!

Worry, like all evils, feeds on itself, and grows greater by its own exercise. Did it decline when exercised, diminish when allowed a free course, one might let it alone, even encourage it, in order that it might the sooner be dead. But, unfortunately, it works the other way. The more one worries the more he continues to worry. The more he yields to it the greater becomes its power. It is a species of hypnotism: once allow it to control, each new exercise diminishes the victim's power of resistance.

Never was monster more cruel, more relentless, more certain to hang on to the bitter end than worry. He shows no mercy, has not the slightest spark of relenting or yielding. And his power is all the greater because it is so subtle. He wants you to be "careful" - taking good care, however, not to let you know that he means to make you *full of care*. He pleads "love" as the cause for his existence. He would have you love your child, hence "worry" about him. He thus trades on your affection to blind you to your child's best interests by "worrying" about him. For when worry besets you, is harassing you on every hand, how can you possibly devote your wisdom, your highest intelligence to safeguarding the welfare of the one you love.

Never was a slave in the South, though in the hands of a Legree, more to be pitied than the slave of worry. He dogs every footstep, is vigilant every moment. He never sleeps, never tires, never relaxes, never releases his hold so long as it is possible for him to retain it. When you seek to awaken people to the terror, the danger, the hourly harm their slavery to worry is bringing to them, they are so completely in worry's power that they weakly respond: "But I can't help it." And they verily believe they can't; that their bondage is a natural thing; a state "ordained from the foundation of the world," altogether ignoring the frightful reflection such a belief is upon the goodness of God and his fatherly care for his children. Natural! It is the most unnatural thing in existence. Do the birds worry? The beasts of the field? The clouds? The winds? The sun, moon, stars, and comets? The trees? The flowers? The rain-drops? How Bryant rebukes the worrier in his wonderful poem "*To a Water Fowl*," and Celia Thaxter in her "*Sandpiper*." The former sings of the fowl winging its solitary way where "rocking billows rise and sink on the chafed ocean-side," yet though "lone wandering" it is not lost. And from its protection he deduces the lesson:

> He who, from zone to zone,
> Guides through the boundless sky thy certain flight,
> In the long way that I must tread alone
> Will lead my steps aright.

And so Celia Thaxter sang of the sandpiper:

> He has no thought of any wrong,
> He scans me with a fearless eye.

And her faith expressed itself in a later verse:

> I do not fear for thee, though wroth
> The tempest rushes through the sky:
> For are we not God's children both,
> Thou, little sandpiper, and I?

There is no worry in Nature. It is man alone that worries. Nature goes on her appointed way each day unperturbed, unvexed, care-free, doing her allotted tasks and resting absolutely in the almighty sustaining power behind her. Should man do any less? Should man - the reasoning creature, with intelligence to see, weigh, judge, appreciate, - alone be uncertain of the fatherly goodness of God; alone be unable to discern the wisdom and love behind all things? Worry, therefore, is an evidence that we do not trust the all-fatherliness of God.

It is also the direct product of vanity, pride and self-conceit. If these three qualities of evil in the human heart could be removed a vast aggregate amount of worry would die instantly. No one can study his fellow creatures and not soon learn that an immense amount of worry is caused by these three evils.

We are worried lest our claims to attention are not fully recognized, less our worth be not observed, our proper station accorded to us. How we press our paltry little claims upon others, how we glorify our own insignificant deeds; how large loom up our small and puny acts. The whole universe centers in us; our ego is a most important thing; our work of the highest value and significance; our worth most inestimable.

The fact of the matter is most men and women are inestimable, their deeds of value, their lives of importance. Our particular circle needs us, as we need those who compose it, we are all important, but few, indeed, are there, whose power, influence and importance reach far. Most of the men and women of the world are ordinary. A man may be a king in Wall street, and yet influence but few outside of his own immediate sphere. Most probably he is unknown to the great mass of mankind. Adventitious circumstances bring some men and women more prominently before the world than others, but even such fame as this is transient, evanescent, and of little importance. The devoted love of our own small circle; the reliable friendship of the few; the blind adoration of the pet dog are worth more than all the "fame," the "eclat," the "renown" of the multitude. And where we have such love, friendship, and blind adoration, let us rest content therein, and smile at the floods of temporary and evanescent emotion which sweep over the mob, but do not have us for their object. I have just read a letter which perfectly illustrates how our vanity, our pride, and personal importance bring much worry to us. The writer - practically a stranger coming from a far-away state - evidently expected to be received with a cordial welcome and open arms, by one who scarcely knew him, given an important place in a lengthy program where men of national reputation were to speak, and generally be treated with deference and respect. Unfortunately his name was not placed *in full* on the program, - curtly initialed he called it - and owing to its length "the chairman caused me to spoil my remarks by asking me to shorten them," and a hotel clerk "outrageously insulted" him when he asked for information. Then, to make ill matters worse - piling Ossa. upon Pelion - he was asked to speak at a certain club, with others. One of the newspapers, in reporting the event, commented upon what the others said and did but ignore him. This he thought might have been merely an oversight, but when, the next day, he saw another report wherein he was not mentioned he was certain "it was a deliberate intention to ignore" him. He then asks that the person to whom he writes "try to find out who is responsible for this affront," and tell him - in order that he may worry some more, I suppose, over trying to "get back at him."

Poor, poor fellow, how he is to be pitied for being so "sensitive," so sure that people regard him enough to want to affront him.

Here is a perfect illustration of the worries caused by vanity; five complaints in one letter, of indignities, or affronts, that an ordinary, robust red-blooded man would have passed by without notice. If I were to worry over the times I have been ignored and neglected I should worry every day. I am fairly well known to many hundreds of thousands of people who read my books, my magazine articles, and hear my lectures, yet I often go to cities and there are no brass bands, no committee, flowers, or banquet to welcome me. No! indeed, the indignity is thrust upon me of having to walk to the hotel, carry my own grip, and register, the same as any other ordinary, common, everyday man! Why should not my blood boil when I think of it? Then, too, when I recall how often my addresses are ignored in the local press, ought not I to be aroused to fierce ire? When a hotel clerk fails to recognize my national importance and gives me a flippant answer when I ask for information should I not deem it time that the Secretary of State interfere and write a State paper upon the matter?

Oh vanity, conceit, pride, how many sleepless hours of worry and fret you bring to your victims, and the pitiable, the lamentable thing about it all is that they congratulate themselves upon being filled with "laudable pride," "recognizing their own importance," and knowing that "honorable ambition" is beneficial. Nothing that causes unnecessary heart-aches and worry is worth while, and of all the prolific causes of these woes commend me to the vanity, the conceit, the pride of small minds and petty natures.

False pride leads its victim to want to make a false impression. He puts on a false appearance. He wishes to appear wiser, better, in easier circumstances, richer than he is. He wears a false front. He is unnatural. He dare not - having decided to make the appearance, and win the impression of falseness - be natural. Hence he is self-conscious all the time lest he make a slip, contradict himself, lose the result he is seeking to attain. He is to be compared to an actor whose part requires him to wear a wig, a false moustache, a false chin. In the hurry of preparation these shams are not adjusted properly and the actor rushes on the stage fearful every moment lest his wig is awry, his moustache fall off, or the chin slip aside and make him ridiculous. He dare not stop to make sure, to "fix" them if they are wrong, as that would reveal their falsity immediately. He can only play on, sweating blood the while.

In the case of the actor one can laugh at the temporary fear and worry, but what a truly pitiable object is the man, the woman, whose whole life is one dread worry lest his, her, false appearance be discovered. And while pride and vanity are not the only sources of these attempts to make false impressions upon others they are a most prolific source. In another chapter I have treated more fully of this phase of the subject.

Wastefulness, extravagance, is a prolific source of worry. Spend to-day, starve to-morrow. Throw your money to the birds to-day; to-morrow the crow, jay, and vulture will laugh and mock at you. Feast to-day; next week you may starve. Riches take to themselves wings and fly away. No one is absolutely safe, and while many thousands go through life indifferent about their expenditures, wasteful and extravagant and do not seem to be brought to time therefor, it must not be forgotten that tens of thousands start out to do the same thing and fail. What is the result? Worry over the folly of the attempt; worry as to where the necessary things for the future are coming from!

While I would not have the well-to-do feel that they must be niggardly I would earnestly warn them against extravagance, against the acquiring of expensive habits of wastefulness that later on may be chains of a cruel bondage. Why forge fetters upon oneself? Far better be

George Wharton James

free now and thus cultivate freedom for whatever future may come. For as sure as sure can be wilful waste and reckless extravagance now will sometime or other produce worry.

One great, deep, awful source of worry is *our failure to accept the inevitable.* Something happens, - we wilfully shut our eyes to the fact that this something has changed *forever* the current of our lives, and if the new current *seems* evil, if it brings discomfort, separation, change of circumstance, etc., we worry, and worry, and continue to worry. This is lamentably foolish, utterly absurd and altogether reprehensible. Let us resolutely face the facts, accept them, and then reshape our lives, bravely and valiantly, to suit the new conditions.

For instance a friend of mine spent twenty years in the employ of a great corporation. As a reward of faithful service he was finally put in a responsible position as the head of a department. A few months ago he was sent East on a special mission connected with his work. Just before his return the corporation elected a new president, who "shook up" the whole concern, changed around several officials, dismissed others, and in the case of my friend, supplanted him by a new man imported from the East, offering him a subordinate position, but, at the same salary he had before been receiving.

How should this man have treated this settled fixed fact in his life? He had two great broad pathways open to him. In one he would deliberately recognize and accept the changed condition, acquiese in it and live accordingly. It is not pleasant to be supplanted, but if another man is appointed to do the work you have been doing, and your superiors think he can do it better than you have been doing it, then manfully face the facts and accord him the most sincere and hearty support. It may be hard, but our training and discipline, - which means our improvement and advancement - come, not from doing the easy and pleasant things, but from striving, cheerfully and pleasantly to do the arduous and disagreeable ones. The other way open for my friend was to resent the change, accept it with anger, let his vanity be wounded, and begin to worry over it. What would have been the probable result? The moment he began to worry his efficiency would have decreased, and he would thus have prepared himself for another "blow" from his employers, another change less to his advantage, and with a possible reduction in salary. His employers, too, would have pointed to his decreased efficiency - the only thing they consider - as justification for their act.

I would not say that if a man, in such a case as I have described, deems that he has been treated unjustly, should not protest, but, when he has protested, and a decision has been rendered against him let him accept the judgment with serenity, refuse to worry over it, and go to work with loyalty and faithfulness, or else seek new employment.

Even, on the other hand, were he to have been discharged, there could have come no good from yielding to worry. *Accept the inevitable*, do not argue or fret about it, put worry aside, go to work to find a new position, and make what seemed to be an evil the stepping-stone to something better.

Mrs. Jessie Benton Fremont, the wife of the gallant pathfinder, General Fremont, was afflicted with deafness in the later years of her life. She, - the petted and flattered, the caressed and spoiled child of fortune, the honored and respected woman of power and superior ability - deaf, and unable to participate in the conversation going on around her. Many a woman under these conditions, would have become irritable, irascible, and a reviler of Fate. To any woman it would have been a great deprivation, but to one mentally endowed as Mrs. Fremont, it was especially severe. Yet did she "worry" about it? No! bravely, cheerfully, boldly, she *accepted the inevitable*, and in effect defied the deafness that had come to her to destroy her happiness, embitter her life, take away the serenity of her mind and the equipoise of her soul. If there had to be a battle to gain this high plane of acceptance, she fought it out in secret, for her friends and the world never heard a word of a murmur from her. I had the joy of a talk with her about it, for it was a joy to have her make light of her affliction, in the great number of good things wherein God had blessed her. Laughingly she said: "Even in deafness I find many compensations. One is never bored by conversation that is neither intelligent, instructive or interesting. I can go to sleep under the most persistent flood of boredom, and like the proverbial water on a duck's back it never bothers me. Again, I never hear the unpleasant things said about either my friends or my enemies, and what a blessing that is. I am also spared hearing about many of the evils, the disagreeable, the unpleasant and horrible things of life that I cannot change, help, or alleviate, and I am thankful for my ignorance. Then, again, when people say things that I can and do hear - in my trumpet - that I don't think anyone should ever say, I can rebuke them by making them think that I heard them say the very opposite of what they did say, and I smile upon them 'and am a villain still.'"

Charles F. Lummis, the well-known litterateur and organizer of the South-West Museum, of Los Angeles, after using his eyes and brain more liberally than most men do in a lifetime thrice, or four times as long as his, was unfortunately struck blind. Did he "worry" over it, and fret himself into a worse condition? No! not for a moment. Cheerfully he accepted the inevitable, got someone to read and write for him, to guide him through the streets, and went ahead with his work just as if nothing had happened, looking forward to the time when his eyesight would be restored to him and hopefully and intelligently worked to that end. In a year or so he and his friends were made happy by that coming to pass, but even had it not been so, I am assured Dr. Lummis would have faced the inevitable without a whimper, a cry, or a word of worry or complaint.

Those who yield to worry over small physical ills should read his inspiring *My Friend Will*,[A] a personal record of his successful struggle against two severe and prostrating attacks of paralysis. One perusal will show them the folly and futility of worry; a second will shame them because they have so little self-control as to spend their time, strength, and energy in worry; and a third perusal will lead them to drive every fragment of worry out of the hidden recesses of their minds and set them upon a better way - a way of serenity, equipoise, and healthful, strenuous, yet joyous and radiant living.

[Footnote A:*My Friend Will*, by C.F. Lummis, A.C. McClurg Co., Chicago.]

Recently I had a conversation with the former super-intendent of a poor farm, which bears upon this subject in a practical way. In relating some of his experiences he told of a "rough-neck" - a term implying an ignorant man of rude, turbulent, quarrelsome disposition - who had threatened to kill the foreman of the farm. Owing to their irreconcilable differences the rough inmate decided to leave and so informed the superintendent, thus practically dismissing himself from the institution. A year later he returned and asked to be re-admitted. After a survey of the whole situation the super-intendent decided that it was not wise to re-admit him, and that he would better secure a situation for him outside. He offered to do so and the man left apparently satisfied. Three days later he reappeared, entered the office with a loaded and cocked revolver held behind his back, and abruptly announced: "I've come to blow out your brains." Before he could shoot the superintendent was upon him and a fierce struggle ensued for the possession of the weapon. The superintendent at last took it away, secured help and handcuffed the would-be murderer. Realizing that his act was the result of at least partial insanity, the was-to-be victim did not press the charge of murderous assault but allowed - indeed urged that he be sent to the insane asylum where he now is.

Now this is the point I wish to make. It is perfectly within the bounds of possibility that this man will some day be regarded as safely sane. Yet it is well known by the awful experiences of many such cases that it is both possible and probable that during the months or years of his incarceration he will continue to harbor, even to feed and foster the bitter feeling, the hatred, perhaps, that led him to attempt the murder of the superintendent, and that on his release he will again attempt to carry out his nefarious and awful design.

What, then, should be the mental attitude of the superintendent and his family? Ought they not to be worried? I got the answer for my readers from this man, and it is so perfectly in accord with my own principles that I find great pleasure in recording it. Said he:

Don't think for one moment that I minimize the possible danger. The asylum physician who was familiar with the whole circumstances warned me not to rest in fancied security. I have notified the proper officials that the man who attempted to murder me is not to be released either as cured or on parole without giving me sufficient notice. I do not wish that he should be kept in the asylum a single day longer than is fully necessary, but before I allow him to be released I must be thoroughly satisfied that he has no murderous designs on me, and that he is truly and satisfactorily repentant for the attack he made when, ostensibly, he was mentally irresponsible. I shall require that he be put on record as fully understanding and appreciating his own personal responsibility for my safety - so that should he still hold any wrongful designs, and afterwards succeed in carrying them out, he or his attorneys will be debarred from again pleading insanity or mental incompetency.

Hence while I fully realize the possibility of danger I do not have a moment's worry about it. I have done and shall do all I can, satisfactorily, to protect myself, without any feeling of harshness or desire to injure the poor fellow, and there I let the matter rest to take care of itself.

This is practical wisdom. This is sane philosophy. Not ignoring the danger, pooh-pooing it, scoffing at it and refusing to recognize it, but calmly, sanely, with a kindly heart looking at possible contingencies, preparing for them, and then serenely trusting to the spiritual forces of life to control events to a wise and satisfactory issue.

Can you suggest anything better? Is not such a course immeasurably better than to allow himself to worry, and fret and fear all the time? Practical precaution, *taken without enmity* - note these italicized words - trustful serenity, faithful performance of present duty unhampered by fears and worries - this is the rational, normal, philosophic, sane course to follow.

Another great source of worry is *our failure to distinguish essentials from non-essentials*. What are the essentials for life? For a man, honesty, truth, earnestness, strength, health, ability to work, and work to do. He may or may not be handsome; he may or may not have wealth, position, fame, education; but to be a man among men, these other things he must have. For a woman, - health, love, work, and such virtues as both men and women need. She might enjoy friends, but they are not essential as health or work; she would be a strange woman if she did not prize beauty, but devoted love is worth far more than beauty or all the conquests it brings. What is the essential for a chair? - its capacity to be used to sit upon with comfort. A house? - that it is adapted to the making of a home. You don't buy a printing-press to curl your hair with but to print, and in accordance with its printing power is it judged. A boat's usefulness is determined by its worthiness in the water, to carry safely, rapidly, largely as is demanded of it.

This is the judgement sanity demands of everything.

What is essential - What not? Is it essential to be a society leader, to belong to every club, to hold office, to give as many dinners as one's neighbors, to have a bigger house, furniture with brighter polish, bigger carvings and more ugly designs than anyone else in town, to have our names in the papers oftener than others, to have more servants, a newer style automobile, put on more show, pomp, ceremony and circumstance than our friends?

By no means! Oh for men and women who have the discerning power - the sight for the essential things, the determination to have them and let non-essentials go. They are the wise ones, the happy ones, the free-from-worry ones.

Later I shall refer extensively to Mrs. Canfield's book *The Squirrel Cage*. She has many wise utterances on this phase of the worry question. For instance, in referring to the mad race for wealth and position that keeps a man away from home so many hours of the day that his wife and child scarce know him she introduces the following dialogue:

> One of them whose house isn't far from mine, told me that he hadn't seen his children, except asleep, for three weeks.
>
> 'But something ought to be done about it!' The girl's deep-lying instinct for instant reparation rose up hotly.
>
> 'Are they so much worse off than most American business men?' queried Rankin. 'Do any of them feel they can take the time to see much more than the outside of their children; and isn't seeing them

asleep about as -'

Lydia cut him short quickly. 'You're always blaming them for that,' she cried. 'You ought to pity them. They can't help it. It's better for the children to have bread and butter, isn't it -'

Rankin shook his head. 'I can't be fooled with that sort of talk - I've lived with too many kinds of people. At least half the time it is not a question of bread and butter. It's a question of giving the children bread and butter and sugar rather than bread and butter and father. Of course, I'm a fanatic on the subject. I'd rather leave off even the butter than the father - let alone the sugar.'

Later on Lydia herself lost her father and after his death her own wail was: 'I never lived with my father. He was always away in the morning before I was up. I was away, or busy, in the evening when he was there. On Sundays he never went to church as mother and I did - I suppose now because he had some other religion of his own. But if he had I never knew what it was - or anything else that was in his mind or heart. It never occurred to me that I could. He tried to love me - I remember so many times now - and *that* makes me cry! - how he tried to love me! He was so glad to see me when I got home from Europe - but he never knew anything that happened to me. I told you once before that when I had pneumonia and nearly died mother kept it from him because he was on a big case. It was all like that - always. He never knew.'

Dr. Melton broke in, his voice uncertain, his face horrified: 'Lydia, I cannot let you go on! you are unfair - you shock me. You are morbid! I knew your father intimately. He loved you beyond expression. He would have done anything for you. But his profession is an exacting one. Put yourself in his place a little. It is all or nothing in the law - as in business.'

But Lydia replied: 'When you bring children Into the world, you expect to have them cost you some money, don't you? You know you mustn't let them die of starvation. Why oughtn't you to expect to have them cost you thought, and some sharing of your life with them, and some time - real time, not just scraps that you can't use for business?'

She made the same appeal once to her husband in regard to their own lives. She wanted to see and know more of him, his business, his inner life, and this was her cry: 'Paul, I'm sure there's something the matter with the way we live - I don't like it! I don't see that it helps us a bit - or anyone else - you're just killing yourself to make money that goes to get things we don't need nearly as much as we need more of each other! We're not getting a bit nearer to each other - actually further away, for we're both getting different from what we were without the other's knowing how! And we're not getting nicer - and what's the use of living if we don't do that? We're just getting more and more set on scrambling ahead of other people. And we're not even having a good time out of it! And here is Ariadne - and another one coming - and we've nothing to give them but just this - this - this -

Paul laughed a little impatiently, irritated and uneasy, as he always was at any attempt to examine too closely the foundations of existing ideas. 'Why, Lydia, what's the matter with you? You sound as though you'd been reading some fool socialist literature or something.'

You know I don't read anything, Paul. I never hear about anything but novels. I never have time for anything else, and very likely I couldn't understand it if I read it, not having any education. That's one thing I want you to help me with. All I want is a chance for us to live together a little more, to have a few more thoughts in common, and oh! to be trying to be making something better out of ourselves for our children's sake. I can't see that we're learning to be anything but -you, to be an efficient machine for making money, I to think of how to entertain as though we had more money than we really have. I don't seem really to know you or live with you any more than if we were two guests stopping at the same hotel. If socialists are trying to fix things better, why shouldn't we have time - both of us - to read their books; and you could help me know what they mean?'

Paul laughed again, a scornful, hateful laugh, which brought the color up to Lydia's pale face like a blow. 'I gather, then, Lydia, that what you're asking me to do is to neglect my business in order to read socialistic literature with you?'

His wife's rare resentment rose. She spoke with dignity: 'I begged you to be serious, Paul, and to try to understand what I mean, although I'm so fumbling, and say it so badly. As for its being impossible to change things, I've heard you say a great many times that there are no conditions that can't be changed if people would really try -'

'Good heavens! I said that of *business* conditions!' shouted Paul, outraged at being so misquoted.

'Well, if it's true of them - No; I feel that things are the way they are because we don't really care enough to have them some other way. If you really cared as much about sharing a part of your life with me - really sharing - as you do about getting the Washburn contract -'

Her indignant and angry tone, so entirely unusual, moved Paul, more than her words, to shocked protest. He looked deeply wounded, and his accent was that of a man righteously aggrieved. 'Lydia, I lay most of this absurd outbreak to your nervous condition, and so I can't blame you for it. But I can't help pointing out to you that it is entirely uncalled for. There are few women who have a husband as absolutely devoted as yours. You grumble about my not sharing my life with you - why, I *give* it to you entire!' His astonished bitterness grew as he voiced it. 'What am I working so hard for if not to provide for you and our child - our children! Good Heavens! What more *can* I do for you than to keep my nose on the grindstone every minute. There are limits to even a husband's time and endurance and capacity for work.'

Hence it will be seen that I would have one Quit Worrying about the non-essentials of life, and this is best done by giving full heed to the essentials and letting the others go. Naturally, if one willfully and purposefully determines to follow non-essentials, he may as well recognize the fact soon as late that he has deliberately chosen a course that cannot fail to produce its own many and irritating worries.

Another serious cause of worry is bashfulness. One who is bashful finds in his intercourse with his fellows many worries. His hands and feet are too large, he blushes at a word, he doesn't know what to say or how, he is confused if attention is directed his way, his thoughts fly to the ends of the earth the moment he is addressed, and if he is expected to say anything, his worries increase so that his pain and distress are manifest to all. To such an one I would say: Assert your manhood, your womanhood. Brace up. Face the music. Remember these facts. You are dealing with men and women, youths and maidens, of the same flesh and blood, mentality as yourself. You average up with the rest of them. Why should you be afraid? Call upon your reasoning power. Assert the dignity of your own existence. You are here by the will of God as much as they. There is a purpose in your creation as much as in theirs. You have a right to be seen and heard as well as have they. Your life may be charged with importance to mankind far more than theirs. Anyhow for what it is, large or small, you are going to use it to the full, and you do not propose to be laughed out of it, sneered out of it, either by the endeavors of others or by your own fears of others. Then, when you have once fully reasoned the thing out, do not hesitate to plunge into the fullest possible association with your fellows. Brave them, defy them (in your own heart), resolutely face them, and my word and assurance for it, they will lose their terror, and you will lose your bashfulness with a speed that will astonish you.

Closely allied to bashfulness as a cause of many worries is hyper-or super-sensitiveness. And yet it is an entirely different mental attitude. Hyper-sensitiveness may cause bashfulness, but there are many thousands of hyper-sensitives who have not a spark of bashfulness in their condition. They are full of vanity or self-conceit. Elsewhere I have referred to one of these. Or they are hyper-sensitive in regard to their health. They mustn't do this, or that, or the other, they must be careful not to sit near a window, allow a door to be open, or go into an unwarmed room. Their feet must never be wet, or their clothing, and as for sleeping in a cold room, or getting up before the fire is lighted, they could not live through such awful hardships.

I have no desire to excoriate or make fun of those who really suffer from chronic invalidism, yet I am fully assured that much of the hyper-sensitiveness of the neurasthenic and hypochondriac could be removed by a little rude, rough and tumble contact with life. It would do most of these people no harm to follow the advice given by Abernethy, the great English physician, to a pampered, overfed hyper-sensitive: Live on six pence a day *and earn it*. I have found few hyper-sensitives among the poor. Poverty is a fine cure for most cases, though there are those who cling to their pride of birth of education, or God knows what of insane belief in their superiority over ordinary mortals, and make that the occasion, or cause, of the innumerable and fretting worries of hyper-sensitiveness.

Another serious cause of worry, in this busy, bustling, rapid age, is the need we feel for hurry. We are caught in the mad rush and its influence leads us to feel that we, too, must rush. There is no earthly reason for our hurry, and yet we cannot seem to help it.

Hurry means worry. Rush spells fret. Haste makes

waste. You live in the country and are a commuter. You must be in the city on the stroke of nine. To do this, you must catch the 8:07. You have your breakfast to get and it takes six minutes to walk to the station. No one can do it comfortably in less. Yet every morning, ever since you took this country cottage, you have had to rush through your breakfast, and rush to the depot in order to catch the train. Thus starting the day on the rush, you have continued "on the stretch" all day, and get back home at night tired out, fretted and worried "almost to death." Even when you sit down to breakfast, you begin to worry if wifie doesn't have everything ready. You know you'll be late. You feel it, and if the toast and coffee are not on the table the moment you sit down, your querelous complaints strike the morning air.

Now what's the use?

Why don't you get up ten, fifteen, or twenty minutes earlier, and thus give yourself time to eat comfortably, and thus get over the worry of your rush? Set the alarm clock for 7:00, or 6:45, or even 6:30. Far better get up half an hour too early, than worry yourself, your wife, and the whole household by your insane hurry. Your worry is wholly unnecessary and shows a fearful lack of simple intelligence.

Annie Laurie, who writes many sage counsels in the *San Francisco Examiner*, had an excellent article on this subject in the issue of December 31, 1915. She wrote:

Here is something that I saw out my window - it has given me the big thought for my biggest New Year's resolution. The man at the corner house ran down the steps in a terrible hurry. He saw the car coming up the hill and whistled to it from the porch, but the man who was running the car did not hear the whistle. Anyway, he didn't stop the car, and the man on the steps looked as if he'd like to catch the conductor of that car and do something distinctly unfriendly to him, and do it right then and there. He jammed his hat down over his forehead and started walking very fast.

"What's your hurry?" said the man he was passing on the corner. "What's your hurry, Joe?" and the man on the corner held out his hand.

"Well, I'll be -," said Joe, and he held out his hand, too, "if it isn't -"

And it was, and they both laughed and shook hands and clapped each other on the back and shook hands again.

"What's your hurry?" said the man on the corner again.

"I dun-no," said the man who was so cross because he'd lost his car. "Nothing much, I guess," and he laughed and the other man laughed and they shook hands again. And the last I saw of them they had started down the street right In the opposite direction from which the man in the hurry had started to go, and they weren't in a hurry at all.

Do you know what I wished right then and there? I wished that every time I get into the senseless habit of rushing everywhere and tearing through everything as if it was my last day on earth and there wasn't a minute left to lose, somebody would stop me on the corner of whatever street of circumstance I may be starting to cross and say to me in friendly fashion:

"What's the hurry?"

What is the hurry, after all? Where are we all going? What for?

What difference does it make whether I read my paper at 8 o'clock in the morning or at half-past 9?

Will the world stop swinging in its orbit if I don't meet just so many people a day, write so many letters, hear so many lectures, skim through so many books? Of course if I'm earning my living I must work for it and work not only honestly but hard. But it seems to me that most of the terrific hurrying we do hasn't much to do with really essential work after all. It's a kind of habit we get into, a sort of madness, like the thing that overtakes the crowd at a ferry landing or the entrance to a train. I've seen men, and women, too, fairly fight to get onto a particular car when the next car would have done just exactly as well.

Where are they going in such a hurry? To save a life? To mend a broken heart? To help to heal a wounded spirit? Or are they just rushing because the rest do it?

What do they get out of life - these people who are always in a rush?

Look! The laurel tree in my California garden is full of bursting buds! The rains are beginning and the trees will soon be flecked with a silver veil of blossoms. I hadn't noticed it before. I've been too busy.

What's your hurry? Come, friend of my heart, I'll say

that to you to-day and say it in deep and friendly earnest.

What's your hurry? Come, let's go for a walk together and see if we can find out. Let us keep finding out through all the new year.

There are many other causes of worry, some of them so insidious, so powerful, as to call for treatment in special chapters.

CHAPTER VIII

PROTEAN FORMS OF WORRY

In a preceding chapter, I have shown that worry is a product of our modern civilization, and that it belongs only to the Occidental world. It is a modern disease, prevalent only among the so-called civilized peoples. There is no doubt that in many respects we *are* what we call ourselves - the most highly civilized people in the world. But do we not pay too high a price for much of our civilization? If it is such that it fails to enable us to conserve our health, our powers of enjoyment, our spontaneity, our mental vigor, our spirituality, and the exuberant radiance of our life - bodily, mental, spiritual - I feel that we need to examine it carefully and find out wherein lies its inadequacy or its insufficiency.

While our civilization has reached some very elevated points, and some men have made wonderful advancement in varied fields, it cannot be denied that the mass of men and women are still groping along in the darkness of mental mediocrity, and on the mud-flats of the commonplace. Ten thousand men and women can now read where ten alone read a few centuries ago. But what are the ten thousand reading? That which will elevate, improve, benefit? See the piles of sensational yellow novels, magazines, and newspapers that deluge us day by day, week by week, month by month, for the answer. True, there are many who desire the better forms of literature, and for these we give thanks; they are of the salt that saves our civilization.

I do not wish to seem, even, to be cynical or pessimistic, but when I look at some of the mental pabulum that our newspapers supply, I cannot but feel that we are making vast efforts to maintain the commonplace and dignify the trivial.

For instance: Look at the large place the Beauty Department of a newspaper occupies in the thoughts of thousands of women and girls. Instead of seeking to know what they should do to keep their bodies and minds healthful and vigorous, they are deeply concerned over their physical appearance. They write and ask questions that show how worried they are about their skin - freckles, pimples, discolorations, patches, etc. - their complexion, their hair, its color, glossiness, quantity, how it should be dressed, and a thousand and one things that clearly reveal the *improper emphasis* placed upon them. I do not wish to ignore the basic facts behind these anxious question-nings. It is right and proper that women (and men also) should give due attention to their physical appearance. But when it becomes a mere matter of the *outward* show of cosmetics, powders, rouges, washes, pencils, and things that affect the outside only, then the emphasis is in the wrong place, and we are worrying about the wrong thing. Our appearance is mainly the result of our physical and mental condition. If the body is healthy, the skin and hair will need no especial attention, and, indeed, every wise person knows that the application of many of the cosmetics, etc., commonly used, is injurious, if not positively dangerous.

George Wharton James

Then, too, observation shows that too many women and girls go beyond reasonable attention to these matters and begin to worry over them. Once become slaves to worry, and every hour of the day some new irritant will arise. Some new "dope" is advertised; some new fashion devised; some new frivolity developed. Vanity and worry now begin to vie with each other as to which shall annoy and vex, sting and irritate their victim the more. Each is a nightmare of a different breed, but no sooner does one bound from the saddle, before the other puts in an appearance and compels its victim to a performance. Only a thorough awakening can shake such nightmares off, and comparatively few have any desire to be awakened. I have watched such victims and they arouse in me both laughter and sadness. One is sure her hair is not the proper color to match her complexion and eyes. It must be dyed. Then follows the worries as to what dye she shall use, and methods of application. Invariably the results produce worry, for they are never satisfactory, and now she is worried while dressing, while eating, and when she goes out into the street, lest people notice that her hair is improperly dyed. Every stranger that looks at her adds to the worry, for it confirms her previous fears that she does not look all right. If she tries another hair of the dog that has already bitten her and allows the hair specialist to guide her again, she goes through more worries of similar fashion. She must treat her hair in a certain way to conform to prevailing styles - and so she worries hourly over a matter that, at the outside, should occupy her attention for a few minutes of each day.

There are men who are equally worried over their appearance. Their hair is not growing properly, or their ears are not the proper shape, or their ears are too large, or their hands are too rough, or their complexion doesn't match the ties they like to wear, or some equally foolish and nonsensical thing. Some wish to be taller, others not so tall; quite an army seeks to be thinner and another of equal numbers desires to be stouter; some wish they were blondes, and others that they were brunettes. The result is that drug-stores, beauty-parlors, and complexion specialists for men and women are kept busy all their time, robbing poor, hard-working creatures of their earnings because of insane worries that they are not appearing as well as they ought to do.

Clothing is a perpetual source of worry to thousands. They must keep up with the styles, the latest fashions, for to be "out of fashion," "a back number," gives them "a conniption fit." An out-of-date hat, or shirt-waist, jacket, coat, skirt, or shoe humiliates and distresses them more than would a violation of the moral law - provided it were undetected.

To these, my worrying friends, I continually put the question: Is it worth while? Is the game worth the shot? What do you gain for all your worry? Rest and peace of mind? Alas, no! If the worry and effort accomplished anything, I would be the last to deprecate it, but observation and experience have taught me that *the more you yield to these demons of vanity and worry, the more relentlessly they harry you.* They veritably are demons that seize you by the throat and hang on like grim death until they suffocate and strangle you.

Do you propose, therefore, any longer to submit? Are you wilfully and knowingly going to allow yourself to remain within their grasp? You have a remedy in your own hands. Kill your foolish vanity by determining to accept yourself as you are. All the efforts in the world will not make any changes worth while. Fix upon the habits of dress, etc., that good sense tells you are reasonable and in accord with your age, your position and your purse, and then follow them regardless of the fashion or the prevailing style. You know as well as I that, unless you are a near-millionaire, you cannot possibly keep up with the many and various changes demanded by current fashion. Then why worry yourself by trying? Why spend your small income upon the unattainable, or upon that which, even if you could attain it, you would find unsatisfying and incomplete?

In your case, worry is certainly the result of mental inoccupancy. This is sometimes called "empty headed-ness," and while the term seems somewhat harsh and rough, it is pretty near the truth. If you spent one-tenth the amount of energy seeking to put something *into* your head that you spend worrying as to what you shall put *on* your head, and how to fix it up, your life would soon be far more different than you can now conceive.

Carelessness and laziness are both great causes of worry. The careless man, the lazy man are each indifferent as to how their work is done; such men seldom do well that which they undertake. Everything carelessly or lazily done is incomplete, inadequate, incompetent, and, therefore, a source of distress, discontent, and worry. A careless or lazy plumber causes much worry, for, even though his victims may have learned the lesson I am endeavoring to inculcate throughout these pages, it is a self-evident proposition that they will not allow his indifferent work to stand without correction. Therefore, the telephone bell calls continually, he or his men must go out and do the work again, and when pay-day comes, he fails to receive the check good work would surely have made forthcoming to him.

The schoolboy, schoolgirl, has to learn this lesson, and the sooner the better. The teacher never nags the careful and earnest student; only the lazy and careless are worried by extra lessons, extra recitals, impositions, and the like.

All through life carelessness and laziness bring worry, and he is a wise person who, as early as he discovers these vices in himself, seeks to correct or, better still, eliminate them.

Another form of worry is that wherein the worrier is sure that no one is to be relied upon to do his duty. Dickens, in his immortal *Pickwick Papers*, gives a forceful example of this type. Mr. Magnus has just introduced himself to Pickwick, and they find they are both going to Norwich on the same stage.

'Now, gen'lm'n,' said the hostler, 'Coach is ready, if you please.'

'Is all my luggage in?' inquired Magnus.

'All right, Sir.'

'Is the red bag in?'

'All right, Sir.'

'And the striped bag?'

'Fore boot, Sir.'

'And the brown-paper parcel?'

'Under the seat, Sir.'

'And the leathern hat-box?'

'They're all in, Sir.'

'Now will you get up?' said Mr. Pickwick.

'Excuse me,' replied Magnus, standing on the wheel. 'Excuse me, Mr. Pickwick, I cannot consent to get up in this state of uncertainty. I am quite satisfied from that man's manner, that that leather hat-box is not in.'

The solemn protestations of the hostler being unavailing, the leather hat-box was obliged to be raked up from the lowest depth of the boot, to satisfy him that it had been safely packed; and after he had been assured on this head, he felt a solemn presentiment, first, that the red bag was mislaid, and next, that the striped bag had been stolen, and then that the brown-paper parcel had become untied. At length when he had received ocular demonstration of the groundless nature of each and every one of these suspicions, he consented to climb up to the roof of the coach, observing that now he had taken everything off his mind he felt quite comfortable and happy.

But this was only a temporary feeling, for as they journeyed along, very break in the conversation was filled up by Mr. Magnus's "loudly expressed anxiety respecting the safety and well-being of the two bags, the leather hat-box, and the brown-paper parcel."

Of course, this is an exaggerated picture, yet it properly suggests and illustrates this particular, senseless form of worry, with which we are all more or less familiar. In business, such a worrier is a constant source of irritation to all with whom he comes in contact, either as inferior or superior. To his inferiors, his worrying is a bedeviling influence that irritates and helps produce the very incapacity for attention to detail that is required; and to superiors, it is a sure sign of incompetency. Experience demonstrates that such an one is incapable of properly directing any great enterprise. Men must be trusted if you would bring out their capacities. Their work should be specifically laid out before them; that is, that which is required of them; not, necessarily, in minute detail, but the general results that are to be achieved. Then give them their freedom to work the problems out in their own way. Give them responsibility, trust them, and then leave them alone. *Quit your worrying* about them. Give them a fair chance, expect, demand results, and if they fail, fire them and get those who are more competent. Mistrust and worry in the employer lead to uncertainty and worry in the employee and these soon spell out failure.

In subsequent chapters, various worries are discussed, with their causes and cures. One thing I cannot too strongly and too often emphasize, and that is, that the more one studies the worries referred to, he is compelled to see the great truth of the proverb, "More of our worries come from within than from without." In other words, we make more of our worries, by worrying, than are made for us by the cares of life.

George Wharton James

This fact in itself should lead us to be suspicious of every worry that besets us.

CHAPTER IX

HEALTH WORRIES

There is an army, whose numbers are legion, who worry about their health and that of the members of their family. What with the doctors scaring the life out of them with the germ theory, seeking to obtain legislation to vaccinate them, examine their children nude in school, take out their tonsils, appendices, and other internal organs, inject serums into them for this, that, and the other, and requiring them to observe a score and one maxims which they do not understand, there is no wonder they are worried. Then when one considers the army of physicians who feel it to be their duty to write of sickness for the benefit of the people, who give detailed symptoms of every disease known; and of the larger army of quacks who deliberately live and fatten themselves upon the worries they can create in the minds of the ignorant, the vicious and the diseased; of the patent-medicine manufacturers, who spend millions of dollars annually in scaring people into the use of their nostrums - none of which are worth the cost of the paper with which they are wrapped up - is there any wonder that people, who are not trained to think, should be worried. Worries meet them on every hand, at every corner. Do they feel an ache or a pain? According to such a doctor, or such a patent-medicine advertisement, that is a dangerous symptom which must be checked at once or the most fearful results will ensue.

Then there are the naturopaths, physicultopaths, gymnastopaths, hygienists, raw food advocates, and a thousand and one other notionists, who give advice as to what, when, and how you shall eat. Horace Fletcher insists that food be chewed until it is liquid; another authority says, "Bosh!" to this and asks you to look at the dog who bolts his meat and is still healthy, vigorous and strong. The raw food advocate assures you that the only good food is uncooked, and that you take out this, that, and the other by cooking, all of which are essential to the welfare of the body. Between these *natural authorities* and the *medical authorities*, there is a great deal of warfare going on all the time, and the layman knows not wherein true safety lies. Is it any wonder that he is worried.

Many members of the medical profession and the drug-stores have themselves to thank for this state of perpetual worriment and mental unrest. They inculcated, nurtured, and fostered a colossal ignorance in regard to the needs of the body, and a tremendous dread and blind fear of everything that seems the slightest degree removed from the everyday normal. They have persistently taught those who rely upon them that the only safe and wise procedure is to rush immediately to a physician upon the first sign of anything even slightly out of the ordinary. Then, with wise looks, mysterious words, strange symbols, and loathsome decoctions, they have sent their victims home to imagine that some marvelous wonder work will follow the swallowing of their abominable mixtures instead of frankly and honestly telling their consultants that their fever was caused by overeating, by too late hours, by dancing in an ill-ventilated room, by too great application to business, by too many cocktails, or too much tobacco smoking.

The results are many and disastrous. People become confirmed "worriers" about their health. On the slightest suspicion of an ache or a pain, they rush to the doctor or the drug-store for a prescription, a dose, a powder, a potion, or a pill. The telephone is kept in constant operation about trivialities, and every month a bill of greater or lesser extent has to be paid.

While I do not wish to deprecate the calling in of a physician in any serious case, by those who deem it advisable, I do condemn as absurd, unnecessary, and foolish in the highest degree, this perpetual worry about trivial symptoms of health. Every truthful physician will frankly tell you - if you ask him - that worrying is often the worst part of the trouble; in other words, that if you never did a thing in these cases that distress you, but would quit your worrying, the discomfort would generally disappear of its own accord.

One result of this kind of worry is that it genders a nervousness that unnecessarily calls up to the mind pictures of a large variety of possible dangers. Who has not met with this nervous species of worrier?

The train enters a tunnel: "What an awful place for a wreck!" Or it is climbing a mountain grade with a deep precipice on one side: "My, if we were to swing off this grade!" I have heard scores of people, who, on riding up the Great Cable Incline of the Mount Lowe Railway, have exclaimed: "What would become of us if this cable were to break?" and they were apparently people of reason and intelligence. The fact is, the cable is so strong and heavy that with two cars crowded to the utmost, their united weight is insufficient to stretch the cable tight, let alone putting any strain upon it sufficient to break it. And most nervous worries are as baseless as this.

"Yet," says some apologist for worries, "accidents do happen. Look at the *Eastland* in Chicago, and the loss of the *Titanic*. Railways have wrecks, collisions, and accidents. Horses do run away. Dogs do bite. People do become sick!"

Granted without debate or discussion. But if everybody on board the wrecked vessels had worried for six months beforehand, would their worries have prevented the wrecks? Mind you, I say worry, not proper precaution. The shipping authorities, all railway officials and employees, etc., should be as alert as possible to guard against all accidents. But this can be done without one moment's worry on the part of a solitary human being, and care is as different from worry as gold is from dross, coal from ashes. By all means, take due precautions; study to avoid the possibility of accidents, but do not give worry a place in your mind for a moment.

A twin brother to this health-worrier is the nervous type, who is sure that every dog loose on the streets is going to bite; every horse driven behind is surely going to run away; every chauffeur is either reckless, drunk, or sure to run into a telegraph pole, have a collision with another car, overturn his car at the corner, or run down the crossing pedestrian; every loitering person is a tramp, who is a burglar in disguise; every stranger is an enemy, or at least must be regarded with suspicion.

Such worriers always seem to prefer to look on the dark side of the unknown rather than on the bright side. "Think no evil!" is good philosophy to apply to everything, as well as genuine religion - when put into practice. The world is in the control of the Powers of Good, and these seek our good, not our disaster. Have faith in the goodness of the powers that be, and work and live to help make your faith true. The man who sees evil where none exists, will do more to call it into existence than he imagines, and equally true, or even more so, is the converse, that he who sees good where none seems to exist, will call it forth, bring it to the surface.

The teacher, who imagines that all children are mean and are merely waiting for a chance to exercise that meanness, will soon justify his suspicions and the children will become what he imagines them to be. Yet such a teacher often little realizes that it has been his own wicked fears and worries that helped - to put it mildly - the evil assert itself.

George Wharton James

CHAPTER X

THE WORRIES OF PARENTS

A worrying parent is at once an exasperating and a pathetic figure. She - for it is generally the mother - is so undeniably influenced by her love that one can sympathize with her anxiety, yet the confidant of her child, or the unconcerned observer is exasperated as he clearly sees the evil she is creating by her foolish, unnecessary worries.

The worries of parents are protean, as are all other worries, and those herein named must be taken merely as suggestions as to scores of others that might be catalogued and described in detail.

Many mothers worry foolishly because their children do not obey, are not always thoughtful and considerate, and act with wisdom, forgetful that life is the school for learning. If any worrying is to be done, let the parent worry over her own folly in not learning how to teach, or train, her child. Line upon line, precept upon precept, here a little, there a little, is the natural procedure with children. It is unreasonable to expect "old heads upon young shoulders." Worry, therefore, that children have not learned before they are taught is as senseless as it is demoralizing. Get down to something practical. I know a mother of a large family of boys and girls. They are as diverse in character and disposition as one might ever find. She is one of the wise, sensible, practical mothers, who acts instead of worrying. For instance, she believes thoroughly in allowing the children to choose their own clothing. It develops judgment, taste, practicability. One of the girls was vain, and always wanted to purchase shoes too small for her, in order that she might have "pretty feet." Each time she brought home small shoes, her mother sent her back with admonitions to secure a larger pair. After this had continued for several times, she decided upon another plan. When the "too small" shoes were brought home, she compelled the girl to wear them, though they pinched and hurt, until they were worn out, and, as she said in telling me the story, "that ended that."

One of her sons was required to get up every morning and light the fire. Very often he was lazy and late so that the fire was not lighted when mother was ready to prepare breakfast. One night he brought home a companion to spend a day or two. The lads frolicked together so that they overslept. When mother got up in the morning, there was no fire. She immediately walked to the foot of the stairs and yelled, "Fire! Fire! Fire!" at the top of her voice. In a few moments, both lads, tousled, half-dressed, and well-scared, rushed downstairs, exclaiming: "Where's the fire? Where's the fire?" "I want it in the stove," was the mother's answer - and "that was the end of that."

The oldest girl became insistent that she be allowed to sit up nights after the others had gone to bed. She would study for awhile and then put her head on her arms and go to sleep. One night her mother waited until she was asleep, went off to bed, and left her. At

George Wharton James

three o'clock in the morning she came downstairs, lighted lamp in hand, and alarm clock set to go off. As soon as the alarm-bell began to ring, the girl awoke, startled to see her mother standing there with the lighted lamp, herself cold and stiff with the discomfort of her position. "And that was the end of that," said the mother.

Here was common-sense, practical, hard-headed training instead of worry. Bend your sense, your intellect, your time, your energy, to seeking how to train your children, instead of doing the senseless, foolish, inane, and utterly useless thing of worrying about them.

Imagine being the child of an anxious parent, who sees sickness in every unusual move or mood of her boy or girl. A little clearing of the throat - "I'm sure he's going to have croup or diphtheria." The girl unconsciously puts her hand to her brow - "What's the matter with your head, dearie; got a headache?" A lad feels a trifle uncomfortable in his clean shirt and wiggles about - "I'm sure Tom's coming down with fever, he's so restless and he looks so flushed!"

God forbid that I should ever appear to caricature the wise care of a devoted mother. That is not what I aim to do. I seek, with intenseness of purpose, to show the folly, the absurdity of the anxieties, the worries, the unnecessary and unreasonable cares of many mothers. For the moment Fear takes possession of them, some kind of nagging is sure to begin for the child. "Oh, Tom, you mustn't do this," or, "Maggie, my darling, you must be careful of that," and the child is not only nagged, but is thus *placed under bondage to the mother's unnecessary alarm.* No young life can suffer this bondage without injury. It destroys freedom and spontaneity, takes away that dash and vigor, that vim and daring that essentially belong to youth, and should be the unhampered heritage of every child. I'd far rather have a boy and girl of mine get sick once in a while - though that is by no means necessary - than have them subjected to the constant fear that they might be sick. And when boys and girls wake up to the full consciousness that their parents' worries are foolish, unnecessary, and self-created, the mental and moral influence upon them is far more pernicious than many even of our wisest observers have perceived.

There never was a boy or girl who was worried over, who was not annoyed, fretted, injured, and cursed by it, instead of being benefited. The benefit received from the love of the parent was in spite of the worry, and not because of it. Worry is a hindrance, a deterrent, a restraint; it is always putting a curbing hand upon the natural exuberance and enthusiasm of youth. It says, "Don't, don't," with such fierce persistence, that it kills initiative, destroys endeavor, murders naturalness, and drives its victims to deception, fraud, and secrecy to gain what they feel to be natural, reasonable and desirable ends.

I verily believe that the parent who forever is saying "Don't" to her children, is as dangerous as a submarine and as cruel as an asphyxiating bomb. Life is for *expression*, not *repression*. Repression is always a proof that a proper avenue for expression has not yet been found. Quit your "don't-ing," and teach your child to "do" right. Children absolutely are taught to dread, then dislike, and finally to hate their parents when they are refused the opportunity of "doing" - of expressing themselves.

Rather seek to find ways in which they may be active. Give them opportunities for pleasure, for employment, for occupation. And remember this, there is as much distance and difference between "tolerating," "allowing," "permitting" your children to do things, and "encouraging," "fostering" in them the desire to do them, as there is distance between the poles. Don't be a dampener to your children, a discourager, a "don'ter," a sign the moment you appear that they must "quit" something, that they must repress their enthusiasm, their fun, their exuberant frolicsomeness, but let them feel your sympathy with them, your comradeship, your good cheer, that "Father, Mother, is a jolly good fellow," and my life for it, you will doubtless save yourself and them much worry in after years.

Hans Christian Andersen's story of *The Ugly Duckling* is one of the best illustrations of the uselessness and needlessness of much of the worry of parents with which I am familiar. How the poor mother duck worried because one of her brood was so large and ugly. At first she was willing to accept it, but when everybody else jeered at it, pushed it aside, bit at it, pecked it on the head, and generally abused it, and the turkey-cock bore down upon it like a ship in full sail, and gobbled at it, and its brothers and sisters hunted it, grew more and more angry with it, and wished the cat would get it and swallow it up, she herself wished it far and far away. And as the worries grew around the poor duckling, it ran away. It didn't know enough to have faith in itself and its own future. The result was the worries of others affected it to the extent of urging it to flee. For the time being this enlarged its worries, until at length, falling in with a band of swans, it felt a strange thrill of fellowship with them in spite of their grand and beautiful appearance, and, soaring into the air after them, it alighted into the water, and seeing its own reflection, was filled with amazement and wonder to find itself no longer an ugly duckling but - a swan.

Many a mother, father, family generally, have worried over their ugly duckling until they have driven him, her, out into the world, only to find out later that their duckling was a swan. And while it was good for the swan to find out its own nature, the points I wish to make are that there was no need for all the worry - it was the sign of ignorance, of a want of perception - and further, the swan would have developed in its home nest just as surely as it did out in the world, and would have been saved all the pain and distress its cruel family visited upon it.

There is still another story, which may as well be introduced here, as it applies to the unnecessary worry of parents about their young. In this case, it was a hen that sat on a nest of eggs. When the chickens were hatched, they all pleased the mother hen but one, and he rushed to the nearest pond, and, in spite of her fret, fuss, fume, and worry, insisted upon plunging in. In vain the hen screamed out that he would drown, her unnatural child was resolved to venture, and to the amazement of all, he floated perfectly, for he was a duck instead of a chicken, and his egg was placed under the old hen by mistake.

Mother, father, don't worry about your child. It may be he is a swan; he may be a duck, instead of the creature you anticipated. Control your fretfulness and your worry for it cannot possibly change things. Wait and watch developments and a few days may reveal enough to you to show you how totally unnecessary all your worries would have been. Teach yourself to know that worry is evil thought directed either upon our own bodies or minds, or those of others. Note, I say *evil* thought. It is not good thought. Good thought so directed would be helpful, useful, beneficial. This is injurious, harmful, baneful. Evil thought, worry, directs to the person, or to that part of the body considered, an injurious and baneful influence that produces pain, inharmony, unhappiness. It is as if one were to divert a stream of corroding acid upon a sensitive wound, and do it because we wished to heal the wound. Worry never once healed a wound, or cured an ill. It always aggravates, irritates, and, furthermore, helps superinduce the evil the worrier is afraid of. The fact that you worry about these things to which I have referred, that you yield your thoughts to them, and, in your worry, give undue contemplation to them, induces the conditions you wish to avoid or avert. Hence, if you wish your child to be well and strong, brave and courageous, it is the height of cruelty for you to worry over his health, his play, or his exercise. Better by far leave him alone than bring upon him the evils you dread. Who has not observed, again and again, the evil that has come from worrying mothers who were constantly cautioning or forbidding their children to do that which every natural and normal child longs to do? Quit your worrying. Leave your child alone. Better by far let him break a rib, or bruise his nose, than all the time to live in the bondage of your fears.

Elsewhere I have referred to the fact that we often bring upon our loved ones the perils we fear. There is a close connection between our mental states and the objects with which we are surrounded. Or, mayhap, it would be more correct to say that it is our mental condition that shapes the actions of those around us in relation to the things by which they are surrounded. Let me illustrate with an incident which happened in my own observation. A small boy and girl had a nervous, ever worrying mother. She was assured that her boy was bound to come to physical ill, for he was so courageous, so adventuresome, so daring. To her he was the duck instead of the chicken she thought she was hatching out. One day he climbed to the roof of the barn. His sister followed him. The two were slowly, and in perfect security, "inching" along on the comb of the roof, when the mother happened to catch sight of them. With a scream of half terror and half anger, she shouted to them to come down *at once!* Up to that moment, I had watched both children with comfort, pleasure, and assurance of their perfect safety. Their manifest delight in their elevated position, the pride of the girl in her pet brother's courage, and his scarcely concealed surprise and pleasure that she should dare to follow him, were interesting in the extreme. But the moment that foolish mother's scream rent the air, everything changed instanter. Both children became nervous, the boy started down the roof, where he could drop upon a lower roof to safety. His little sister, however, started down too soon. Her mother's fears unnerved her and she slid, and falling some twenty-five feet or so, broke her arm.

Then - and here was the cruel fatuity of the whole proceeding - the mother began to wail and exclaim to the effect that it was just what she expected. May I be pardoned for calling her a worrying fool. She could not see that it was her very expectation, and giving voice to it, in her hourly worryings and in that command that they come down, that caused the accident. She, herself, alone was to blame; her unnecessary worry was the cause of her daughter's broken arm.

Christ's constant incitement to his disciples was "Be not afraid!" He was fully aware of the fact that Job declared: "The thing which I greatly feared is come upon me."

Hence, worrying mother, curb your worry, kill it, drive it out, for *your child's sake*. You claim it is for your child's good that you worry. You are wrong. It is because you are too thoughtless, faithless, and trustless that you worry, and, if you will pardon me, *too selfish*. If, instead of giving vent to that fear, worry, dread, you exercised your reason and faith a little more, and then self-denial, and refused to give vocal expression to your worry, you could then claim unselfishness in the interest of your child. But to put your fears and worries, your dreads and anxieties, around a young child, destroying his exuberance and joy, surrounding him with the mental and spiritual fogs that beset your own life is neither wise, kind, nor unselfish.

Another serious worry that besets many parents is that pertaining to the courtship or engagement of their children. Here again let me caution my readers not to construe my admonitions into indifference to this important epoch in their child's life. I would have them lovingly, wisely, sagely advise. But there is a vast difference between this, and the uneasy, fretful, nagging worries that beset so many parents and which often lead to serious friction. Remember that it is your child, not you, who has to be suited with a life partner. The girl who may call forth his warmest affection may be the last person in the world you would have chosen, yet you are not the one to be concerned.

In the January, 1916, *Ladies' Home Journal* there is an excellent editorial bearing upon this subject, as follows:

A mother got to worrying about the girl to whom her son had become engaged. She was a nice girl, but the mother felt that perhaps she was not of a type to stimulate the son sufficiently in his career. The mother wisely said nothing, however, until two important facts dawned upon her:

First, that possibly her boy was of the order which did not need stimulation. As she reflected upon his nature, his temperament, she arrived at the conclusion that what he required in a life partner might be someone who would prove a poultice rather than a mustard plaster or a fly blister.

This was her first discovery.

The second was not precisely like unto it, but was even more important - that the son, and not the mother, was marrying the girl. The question as to whether or not the girl would suit the mother as a permanent companion was a minor consideration about which she need not vex her soul. The point he had settled for himself was that here, by God's grace, was the one maid for him; and since that had been determined the wise course was for the mother not to waste time and energy bemusing (worrying) herself over the situation, especially as the girl offered no fundamental objections.

Thus the mother, of herself, learned a lesson that many another mother might profitably learn.

How wonderfully in his *Saul* does Robert Browning set forth the opposite course to that of the worrier.

Here, the active principle of love and trust are called upon so that it uplifts and blesses its object. David is represented as filled with a great love for Saul, which would bring happiness to him. He strives in every way to make Saul happy, yet the king remains sad, depressed, and unhappy. At last David's heart and his reason grasp the one great fact of God's transcending love, and the poem ends with a burst of rapture. His discovery is that, if his heart is so full of love to Saul, that in his yearning for his good, he would give him everything, what must God's love for him be? Of his own love he cries:

Could I help thee, my father, inventing a bliss, I would add, to that life of the past, both the future and this;

I would give thee new life altogether, as good, ages hence, At this moment, - had love but the warrant love's heart to dispense.

Then, when God's magnificent love bursts upon him he sings in joy:

- What, my soul? see thus far and no farther? When doors great and small

Nine-and-ninety flew ope at our touch, should the hundredth appall?

How utterly absurd, on the face of it, is such a supposition. God having given so much will surely continue to give. His love so far proven so great, it *will never cease.*

O! doubting heart of man, of woman, of father, of

mother, grieving over the mental and spiritual lapses of a loved one, grasp this glorious fact - God's love far transcends thine own. What thou wouldst do for thy loved one is a minute fraction of what He can do, will do, *is doing*. Rest in His love. He will not fail thee nor forsake thee; and in His hands all whom thou lovest are safe.

CHAPTER XI

MARITAL WORRIES

I now approach a difficult part of my subject, yet I do it without trepidation, fear, or worry as to results. There are, to my mind, a few fundamental principles to be considered and observed, and each married couple must learn to fight the battle out for themselves.

Undoubtedly, to most married people, the ideal relationship is where each is so perfectly in accord with the other - they think alike, agree, are as one mentally - that there are no irritations, no differences of opinion, no serious questions to discuss.

Others have a different ideal. They do not object to differences, serious, even, and wide. They are so thorough believers in the sanctity of the individuality of each person - that every individual must live his own life, and thus learn his own lessons, that what they ask is a love large enough, big enough, sympathetic enough, to embrace all differences, and in confidence that the "working out" process will be as sure for one as the other, to rest, content and serene in each other's love in spite of the things that otherwise would divide them.

This mental attitude, however, requires a large faith in

God, a wonderful belief in the good that is in each person, and a forbearing wisdom that few possess. Nevertheless, it is well worth striving for, and its possession is more desirable than many riches. And how different the outlook upon life from that of the marital worrier. When a couple begin to live together, they have within themselves the possibilities of heaven or of hell. The balance between the two, however, is very slight. There is only a foot, or less, in difference, between the West and the East on the Transcontinental Divide. I have stood with one foot in a rivulet the waters of which reached the Pacific, and the other in one which reached the Atlantic. The marital divide is even finer than that. It is all in the habit of mind. If one determines that he, she, will guide, boss, direct, control the other, one of two or three things is sure to occur.

I. The one mind *will* control the other, and an individual will live some one else's life instead of its own. This is the popular American notion of the life of the English wife. She has been trained during the centuries to recognize her husband as lord and master, and she unquestionably and unhesitatingly obeys his every dictate. Without at all regarding this popular conception as an accurate one, nationally, it will serve the purpose of illustration.

II. The second alternative is one of sullen submission. If one hates to "row," to be "nagged," he, she, submits, but with a bad grace, consumed constantly with an inward rebellion, which destroys love, leads to cowardly subterfuges, deceptions, and separations.

III. The third outcome is open rebellion, and the results of this are too well known to need elucidation - for whatever they may be, they are disastrous to the peace, happiness, and content of the family relationship.

Yet to show how hard it is to classify actual cases in any formal way, let me here introduce what I wrote long ago about a couple whom I have visited many times. It is a husband and wife who are both geniuses - far above the ordinary in several lines. They have money - made by their own work - the wife's as well as the husband's, for she is an architect and builder of fine homes. While they have great affection one for another, there is a constant undertone of worry in their lives. Each is too critical of the other. They worry about trifles. Each is losing daily the sweetness of sympathetic and joyous comradeship because they do not see eye to eye in all things. Where a mutual criticism of one's work is agreed upon, and is mutually acceptable and unirritating, there is no objection to it. Rather should it be a source of congratulation that each is so desirous of improving that criticism is welcomed. But, in many cases, it is a positive and injurious irritant. One meets with criticism, neither kind nor gentle, out in the world. In the home, both man and woman need tenderness, sympathy, comradeship - and if there be weaknesses or failures that are openly or frankly confessed, there should be the added grace and virtue of compassion without any air of pitying conde-scension or superiority. By all means help each other to mend, to improve, to reach after higher, noble things, but don't do it by the way of personal criticism, advice, remonstrance, fault-finding, worrying. If you do, you'll do far more harm than good in ninety-nine cases out of every hundred. Every human being instinctively, in such position, consciously or unconsciously, places himself in the attitude of saying: "I am what I am! Now recognize that, and leave me alone! My life is mine to learn its lessons in my own way, just the same as yours is to learn your lessons in your way." This worrying about, and of each other has proven destructive of much domestic happiness, and has wrecked many a marital barque, that started out with sails set, fair wind, and excellent prospects.

Don't worry about each other - *help* each other by the loving sympathy that soothes and comforts. Example is worth a million times more than precept and criticism, no matter how lovingly and wisely applied, and few men and women are wise enough to criticise and advise *perpetually*, without giving the recipient the feeling that he is being "nagged."

Granted that, from the critic's standpoint, every word said may be true, wise, and just. This does not, by any means, make it wise to say it. The mental and spiritual condition of the recipient *must* be considered as of far more importance than the condition of the giver of the wise exhortations. The latter is all right, he doesn't need such admonitions; the other does. The important question, therefore, should be: "Is he ready to receive them?" If not, if the time is unpropitious, the mental condition inauspicious, better do, say, nothing, than make matters worse. But, unfortunately, it generally happens that at such times the critic is far more concerned at unbosoming himself of his just and wise admonitions than he is as to whether the time is ripe, the conditions the best possible, for the word to be spoken. The sacred writer has something very wise and illuminating to say upon this subject. Solomon says: "A word spoken in due season, how good is it!" Note, however, that it must be spoken "in due season," to be good. The same word spoken out of season may be, and often is, exceedingly bad. Again he says: "A word fitly spoken is like apples of gold in pictures of silver."

But it must be *fitly* spoken to be worthy to rank with apples of gold.

CHAPTER XII

THE WORRY OF THE SQUIRREL CAGE

Reference has already been made to *The Squirrel Cage*, by Dorothy Canfield. Better than any book I have read for a long time, it reveals the causes of much of the worry that curses our modern so-called civilized life. These causes are complex and various. They include *vanity, undue attention to what our neighbors think of us, a false appreciation of the values of things*, and they may all be summed up into what I propose to call - with due acknowledgement to Mrs. Canfield - *the Worry of the Squirrel Cage*.

I will let the author express her own meaning of this latter term. If the story leading up seems to be long please seek to read it in the light of this expression:[A]

[Footnote A: Reprinted from "The Squirrel-Cage" by Dorothy Canfield ($1.35 net); published by Henry Holt and Company, New York City.]

When Mr. and Mrs. Emery, directly after their wedding in a small Central New York village, had gone West to Ohio, they had spent their tiny capital in building a small story-and-a-half cottage, ornamented with the jig-saw work and fancy turning popular in 1872, and this had been the nucleus of their present rambling, picturesque, many-roomed home. Every step in the long series of changes which had led from its first state to its last had a profound and gratifying significance for the Emerys and its final condition, prosperous, modern, sophisticated, with the right kind of wood work in every room that showed, with the latest, most unobtrusively artistic effects in decoration, represented their culminating well-earned position in the inner circle of the best society of Endbury.

Moreover, they felt that just as the house had been attained with effort, self-denial, and careful calculations, yet still without incurring debt, so their social position had been secured by unremitting diligence and care, but with no loss of self-respect or even of dignity. They were honestly proud of both their house and of their list of acquaintances and saw no reason to regard them as less worthy achievements of an industrious life than their four creditable grown-up children or Judge Emery's honorable reputation at the bar.

The two older children, George and Marietta, could remember those early struggling days with as fresh an emotion as that of their parents. Indeed, Marietta, now a competent, sharp-eyed matron of thirty-two, could not see the most innocuous colored lithograph without an uncontrollable wave of bitterness, so present to her mind was the period when they painfully groped their way out of chromos.

The particular Mrs. Hollister who, at the time the Emerys began to pierce the upper crust, was the leader of Endbury society, had discarded chromos as much as five years before. Mrs. Emery and

Marietta, newly admitted to the honor of her acquaintance, wondered to themselves at the cold monotony of her black and white engravings. The artlessness of this wonder struck shame to their hearts when they chanced to learn that the lady had repaid it with a worldly-wise amusement at their own highly-colored waterfalls and snow-capped mountain-peaks. Marietta could recall as piercingly as if it were yesterday, in how crestfallen a chagrin she and her mother had gazed at their parlor after this incident, their disillusioned eyes open for the first time to the futility of its claim to sophistication. As for the incident that had led to the permanent retiring from their table of the monumental salt-and-pepper 'caster' which had been one of their most prized wedding presents, the Emerys refused to allow themselves to remember it, so intolerably did it spell humiliation.

In these quotations the reader has the key to the situation - worry to become as good as one's neighbors, if not better. *This is the worry of the squirrel cage.*

Lydia is Mrs. Emery's baby girl, her pet, her passionate delight. She has been away to a fine school. She knows nothing of the ancient struggles to attain position and a high place in society. Those struggles were practically over before she appeared on the scene.

On the occasion of her final home-coming her mother makes great preparations to please her, yet the worry and the anxiety, are revealed in her conversation with her older daughter:

'Oh, Marietta, how *do* you suppose the house will seem to Lydia after she has seen so much? I hope she won't be disappointed. I've done so much to it this last year, perhaps she won't like it. And oh, I *was* so tired because we weren't able to get the new sideboard put up in the dining-room yesterday!'

'Really, Mother, you must draw the line about Lydia. She's only human. I guess if the house is good enough for you and father it is good enough for her.'

'That's just it, Marietta - that's just what came over me! *Is* what's good enough for us good enough for Lydia? Won't anything, even the best, in Endbury be a come-down for her?'

The attainments of Mrs. Emery both as to wealth and social position, however, were not reached by her daughter Marietta and her husband, but in the determination to make it appear as if they were, Marietta thus exposes her own life of worry in a talk with her father:

'Keeping up a two-maid and a man establishment on a one-maid income, and mostly not being able to hire the one maid. There aren't *any* girls to be had lately. It means that I have to be the other maid and the man all of the time, and all three, part of the time.' She was starting down the step, but paused as though she could not resist the relief that came from expression. 'And the cost of living - the necessities are bad enough, but the other things - the things you have to have not to be out of everything! I lie awake nights. I think of it in church. I can't think of anything else but the way the expenses mount up. Everybody getting so reckless and extravagant and I *won't* go in debt! I'll come to it, though. Everybody else does. We're the only people that haven't oriental rugs now. Why, the Gilberts - and everybody knows how much they still owe Dr. Melton for Ellen's appendicitis, and their grocer told Ralph they owe him several hundred dollars - well, they have just got an oriental rug that they paid a hundred and sixty dollars for. Mrs. Gilbert said they 'just *had* to have it, and you can always have what you have to have.' It makes me sick! Our parlor looks so common! And the last dinner party we gave cost -'

Another phase of the *squirrel cage worry* is expressed in this terse paragraph:

'Father keeps talking about getting one of those player-pianos, but Mother says they are so new you can't tell what they are going to be. She says they may get to be too common.'

Bye and bye it comes Lydia's turn to decide what place she and her new husband are to take in Endbury society, and here is what one frank, sensible man says about it:

'It may be all right for Marietta Mortimer to kill herself body and soul by inches to keep what bores her to death to have - a social position in Endbury's two-for-a-cent society, but, for the Lord's sake, why do they make such a howling and yelling just at the tree when Lydia's got the tragically important question to decide as to whether that's what *she* wants? It's like expecting her to do a problem in calculus in the midst of an earthquake.'

And the following chapter is a graphic presentation as

to how Lydia made her choice "in perfect freedom" - oh, the frightful sarcasm of the phrase - during the excitement of the wedding preparations and under the pressure of expensive gifts and the ideas of over enthusiastic "society" friends.

Lydia now began her own "squirrel-cage" existence, even her husband urges her into extravagance in spite of her protest by saying, "Nothing's too good for you. And besides, it's an asset. The mortgage won't be so very large. And if we're in it, we'll just have to live up to it. It'll be a stimulus."

One of the sane characters of the book is dear, lovable, gruff Mr. Melton, who is Lydia's godfather, and her final awakening is largely due to him. One day he finds Lydia's mother upstairs sick-a-bed, and thus breaks forth to his godchild:

'About your mother - I know without going upstairs that she is floored with one or another manifestation of the great disease of *social-ambitionitis*. But calm yourself. It's not so bad as it seems when you've got the right doctor, I've practiced for thirty years among Endbury ladies. They can't spring anything new on me. I've taken your mother through doily fever induced by the change from tablecloths to bare tops, through portiere inflammation, through afternoon tea distem-per, through *art-nouveau* prostration and mission furniture palsy, not to speak of a horrible attack of acute insanity over the necessity of having her maids wear caps. I think you can trust me, whatever dodge the old malady is working on her.'

And later in speaking of Lydia's sister he affirms:

'Your sister Marietta is not a very happy woman. She has too many of your father's brains for the life she's been shunted into. She might be damming up a big river with a finely constructed concrete dam, and what she is giving all her strength to is trying to hold back a muddy little trickle with her bare hands. The achievement of her life is to give on a two-thousand-a-year income the appearance of having five thousand like your father. She does it; she's a remarkably forceful woman, but it frets her. She ought to be in better business, and she knows it, though she won't admit it.'

Oh, the pity of it, the woe of it, the horror of it, for it is one of the curses of our present day society and is one of the causes of many a man's and woman's physical and mental ruin. In the words of our author elsewhere:

They are killing themselves to get what they really don't want and don't need, and are starving for things they could easily have by just putting out their hands.

Where life's struggle is reduced to this kind of thing, there is little compensation, hence we are not surprised to read that:

Judge Emery was in the state in which of late the end of the day's work found him - overwhelmingly fatigued. He had not an ounce of superfluous energy to answer his wife's tocsin, while she was almost crying with nervous exhaustion. That Lydia's course ran smooth through a thousand complications was not accomplished without an incalculable expenditure of nervous force on her mother's part. Dr. Melton had several times of late predicted that he would have his old patient back under his care again. Judge Emery, remembering this prophecy, was now moved by his wife's pale agitation to a heart-sickening mixture or apprehension for her and of recollection of his own extreme discomfort whenever she was sick.

Yet in spite of this intense tension, she was unable to stop - felt she must go on, until finally, a breakdown intervened and she was compelled to lay by.

On another page a friend tells of his great-aunt's experience:

'She told me that all through her childhood her family was saving and pulling together to build a fine big house. They worked along for years until, when she was a young lady, they finally accomplished it; built a big three-story house that was the admiration of the countryside. Then they moved in. And it took the womenfolks every minute of their time, and more to keep it clean and in order; it cost as much to keep it up, heated, furnished, repaired, painted and everything the way a fine house should be, as their entire living used to cost. The fine big grounds they had laid out to go with the mansion took so much time to -'

Finally Lydia herself becomes awakened, startled as she sees what everybody is trying to make her life become and she bursts out to her sister:

'I'm just frightened of - everything - what everybody expects me to do, and to go on doing all my life, and never have any time but to just hurry faster and faster, so there'll be more things to hurry about, and never talk about anything but *things!*' She began to tremble and look white, and stopped with a desperate effort to control herself, though she burst out at the sight of Mrs. Mortimer's face of despairing bewilderment. 'Oh, don't tell me you don't see at all what I mean. I can't say it! But you *must* understand. Can't we somehow all stop - now! And start over again! You get muslin curtains and not mend your lace ones, and Mother stop fussing about whom to invite to that party - that's going to cost more than he can afford, Father says - it makes me *sick* to be costing him so much. And not fuss about having clothes just so - and Paul have our house built little and plain, so it won't be so much work to take care of it and keep it clean. I would so much rather look after it myself than to have him kill himself making money so I can hire maids that you *can't* - you say yourself you can't - and never having any time to see him. Perhaps if we did, other people might, and we'd all have more time to like things that make us nicer to like.

And when her sister tried to comfort her she continued:

'You do see what I mean! You see how dreadful it is to look forward to just that - being so desperately troubled over things that don't really matter - and - and perhaps having children, and bringing them to the same thing - when there must be so many things that do matter!'

Then, to show how perfectly her sister understood, the author makes that wise and perceptive woman exclaim:

'Mercy! Dr. Melton's right! She's perfectly wild with nerves! We must get her married as soon as ever we can!'

Lydia gives a reception. Here is part of the description:

Standing as they were, tightly pressed in between a number of different groups, their ears were assaulted by a disjointed mass of stentorian conversation that gave a singular illusion as if it all came from one inconceivably voluble source, the individuality of the voices being lost in the screaming enunciation which, as Mrs. Sandworth had pointed out, was a prerequisite of self-expression under the circumstances.

They heard: *'For over a month and the sleeves were too see you again at Mrs. Elliott's I'm pouring there from four I've got to dismiss one with plum-colored bows all along five dollars a week and the washing out and still impossible! I was there myself all the time and they neither of thirty-five cents a pound for the most ordinary ferns and red carnations was all they had, and we thought it rather skimpy under the brought up in one big braid and caught down with at Peterson's they were pink and white with -'* ... *'Oh, no, Madeleine! that was at the Burlingame's.'* Mrs. Sandworth took a running jump into the din and sank from her brother's sight, vociferating: *'The Petersons had them of old gold, don't you remember, with little -'*

The doctor, worming his way desperately through the masses of femininity, and resisting all attempts to engage him in the local fray, emerged at length into the darkened hall where the air was, as he told himself in a frenzied flight of imagination, less like a combination of a menagerie and a perfume shop. Here, in a quiet corner, sat Lydia's father alone. He held in one hand a large platter piled high with wafer-like sandwiches, which he was consuming at a Gargantuan rate, and as he ate, he smiled to himself.

'Well, Mr. Ogre,' said the doctor, sitting down beside him with a gasp of relief; 'let a wave-worn mariner into your den, will you?'

Provided with an auditor, Judge Emery's smile broke into an open laugh. He waved the platter toward the uproar in the next rooms: 'A boiler factory ain't in it with woman, lovely woman, is it?' he put it to his friend.

'Gracious powers! There's nothing to laugh at in that exhibition!' the doctor reproved him, with an acrimonious savagery. 'I don't know which makes me sicker; to stay in there and listen to them, or come out here and find you thinking they're *funny*!'

They are funny!' insisted the Judge tranquilly. 'I stood by the door and listened to the scraps of talk I could catch, till I thought I should have a fit. I never heard anything funnier on the stage.'

'Looky here, Nat,' the doctor stared up at him angrily, 'they're not monkeys in a zoo, to be looked at only on holidays and then laughed at! They're the other half of a whole that we're half of, and don't you forget it! Why in the world should you think it funny for them to do this tomfool trick all winter and have nervous prostration all summer to pay for it? You'd lock up a *man* as a dangerous lunatic if he spent his life so. What they're like, and what they do with their time and strength concerns us enough sight more than what the tariff is, let me tell you.'

'I admit that what your wife is like concerns you a whole lot!' The Judge laughed good-naturedly in the face of the little old bachelor. 'Don't commence jumping on the American woman so! I won't stand it! She's the noblest of her sex!'

'Do you know why I am bald?' said Dr. Melton, running his hand over his shining dome.

'If I did, I wouldn't admit it,' the Judge put up a cautious guard, 'because I foresee that whatever I say will be used as evidence against me.'

'I've torn out all my hair in desperation at hearing such men as you claim to admire and respect and wish to advance the American woman. You don't give enough thought to her - real thought - from one year's end to another to know whether you think she has an immortal soul or not!'

Later Lydia's husband insists that they give a dinner.

It was to be a large dinner - large, that is, for Endbury - of twenty covers, and Lydia had never prepared a table for so many guests. The number of objects necessary for the conventional setting of a dinner table appalled her. She was so tired, and her attention was so fixed on the complicated processes going on uncertainly in the kitchen, that her brain reeled over the vast quantity of knives and forks and plates and glasses needed to convey food to twenty mouths on a festal occasion. They persistently eluded her attempts to marshal them into order. She discovered that she had put forks for the soup - that in some inexplicable way at the plate destined for an important guest there was a large kitchen spoon of iron, a wild sort of whimsical humor rose in her from the ferment of utter fatigue and anxiety. When Paul came in, looking very grave, she told him with a wavering laugh, 'If I tried as hard for ten minutes to go to Heaven as I've tried all day to have this dinner right, I'd certainly have a front seat in the angel choir. If anybody here to-night is not satisfied, it'll be because he's harder to please than St. Peter himself.'

During the evening:

Lydia seemed to herself to be in an endless bad dream. The exhausting efforts of the day had reduced her to a sort of coma of fatigue through which she felt but dully the successive stabs of the ill-served unsuccessful dinner. At times, the table, the guests, the room itself, wavered before her, and she clutched at her chair to keep her balance. She did not know that she was laughing and talking gaily and eating nothing. She was only conscious of an intense longing for the end of things, and darkness and quiet.

When it was all over and her husband was compelled to recognize that it had been a failure, his mental attitude is thus expressed:

He had determined to preserve at all costs the appearance of the indulgent, non-critical, over-patient husband that he intensely felt himself to be. No force, he thought grimly, shutting his jaws hard, should drag from him a word of his real sentiments.

Fanned by the wind of this virtuous resolution, his sentiments grew hotter and hotter as he walked about, locking doors and windows, and reviewing bitterly the events of the evening. If he was to restrain himself from saying, he would at least allow himself the privilege of feeling all that was possible to a man deeply injured.

And that night Lydia felt for the "first time the quickening to life of her child. And during all that day, until then, she had forgotten that she was to know motherhood." Can words more forcefully depict the *worry of the squirrel-cage* than this - that an unnecessary dinner, given in unnecessary style, at unnecessary expense, to visitors to whom it was unnecessary should have driven from her thought, and doubtless seriously injured, the new life that she was so soon to give to the world?

Oh, men and women of divine descent and divine heritage, quit your squirrel-cage stage of existence. Is life to be one mere whirling around of the cage of useless toil or pleasure, of mere imagining that you are doing something? Work with an object. Know your object, that it is worthy the highest endeavor of a human being, and then pursue it with a divine enthusiasm that no obstacle can daunt, an ardor that no weariness can quench. Then it is you will begin to live. There is no life in *worry*. Worry is a waste of life. If you are a worrier, that is a proof you (in so far as you worry) do not appreciate the value of your own life, for a worthy object, a divine enthusiasm, a noble ardor are in themselves the best possible preventives against worry. They dignify life above worry. Worry is undignified, petty, paltry. Where you know you have something to do worth doing, you are conscious of the

Divine Benediction, and who can worry when the smile of God rests upon him? This is a truism almost to triteness, and yet how few fully realize it. It is the unworthy potterers with life, the dabblers in life-stuff, those who blind themselves to their high estate, those who are unsure of their footing who worry. The true aristocrat is never worried about his position; the orator convinced of the truth of his message worries not as to how it will be received; the machinist sure of his plans hesitates not in the construction of his machinery; the architect assured of his accuracy pushes on his builders without hesitancy or question, fear, or alarm; the engineer knowing his engine and his destination has no heart quiver as he handles the lever. It is the doubter, the unsure, the aimless, the dabbler, the frivolous, the dilettante, the uncertain that worry. How nobly Browning set this forth in his Epilogue:

> What had I on earth to do
> With the slothful, with the mawkish, the unmanly?
> Like the aimless, helpless, hopeless, did I drivel
> - Being - Who?
> One who never turned his back but marched breast forward,
> Never doubted clouds would break,
> Never dreamed, though right were worsted, wrong would triumph,
> Held we fall to rise, are baffled to fight better,
> Sleep to wake.
> No, at noonday in the bustle of man's worktime
> Greet the unseen with a cheer!
> Bid him forward, breast and back as either should be,
> 'Strive and thrive!' cry 'Speed, - fight on, fare ever
> There as here!'

And this is not "mere poetry." Or rather it is because it is "mere poetry" that it is *real life*. Browning had nearly seventy years of it. He knew. Where there are those to whom "God has whispered in the ear," there is no uncertainty, no worry. The musician who knows his instrument, knows his music, knows his key, and knows his time to play never hesitates, never falters, never worries. With tone clear, pure, strong, and certain, he sends forth his melodies or harmonies into the air. Cannot you, in your daily life, be a true and sure musician? Cannot you be *certain* - absolutely, definitely certain - of your right to play the tune of life in the way you have it marked out before you, and then go ahead and play! Play, in God's name, as God's and man's music-maker.

CHAPTER XIII

RELIGIOUS WORRIES AND WORRIERS

Misunderstandings, misconceptions, and ignorance in regard to what really is religion have caused countless millions to mourn - and worry; indeed, far more to worry than to mourn. Religion should be a joyous thing, the bringing of the son and daughter into close relationship with the Father. Instead, for centuries, it has been a battle for creeds, for mental assent to certain doctrines, rather than a growth in brotherhood and loving relationship, and those who could not see eye to eye with one another deemed it to be their duty to fight and worry each other - even to their death.

This is not the place for any theological discussion; nor is it my intent to present the claims of any church or creed. Each reader must do that for himself, and the less he worries over it, the better I think it will be for him. I have read and reread Cardinal Newman's wonderful *Pro Apologia* - his statement as to why and how he entered the bosom of the Roman Catholic Church, and it has thrilled me with its pathos and evidence of deep spiritual endeavor. Charles Warren Stoddard's *Troubled Heart and How It Found Rest* is another similar story, though written by an entirely different type of man. Each of these books revealed the inner thought and life of men who were worried about religion, and by worry I mean anxious to the point of abnormality, disturbed, distressed unnecessarily. Yet I would not be misunderstood. Far be it from me, in this age of gross materialism and worship of physical power and wealth, to decry in the least a proper degree of solicitude for one's personal salvation. The religious life of the individual - the real, deep, personal, hidden, unseen, inner life of a human soul - is a wonderfully delicate thing, to be touched by another only with the profoundest love and deepest wisdom. Hence I have little to say about one's own inner struggles, except to affirm and reaffirm that wisdom, sanity, and religion itself are *all* against worrying about it. Study religion, consider it, accept it, follow it, earnestly, seriously, and constantly, but do it in a rational manner, seeking the essentials, accepting them and then *resting* in them to the full and utter exclusion of all worry.

But there is another class of religious worriers, viz., those who worry themselves about *your* salvation. Again I would not be misunderstood, nor thought to decry a certain degree of solicitude about the spiritual welfare of those we love, but here again the caution and warning against worry more than ever holds good. Most of these worriers have found comfort, joy, and peace in a certain line of thought, which has commended itself to them as *Truth* - the one, full, complete, indivisible Truth, and it seems most natural for human nature to be eager that others should possess it. This is the secret of the zeal of the street Salvationist, whose flaming ardor is bent on reaching those who seldom, if ever, go to church. The burden of his cry is that you must flee from the wrath to come - hell - by accepting the vicarious atonement made by the "blood of Jesus." In season and out of season, he urges that you "come under the blood." His face is tense, his brow wrinkled, his eyes strained, his voice raucous, his whole demeanor full of worry over the salvation of others.

Another friend is a Seventh Day Adventist, who is full of zeal for the declaration of the "Third Angel's Message," for he believes that only by heeding it, keeping sacred the hours from sunset on Friday to Saturday sunset, in accordance with his reading of the fourth commandment, and also believing in the speedy second coming of Christ, can one's soul's salvation be attained.

The Baptist is assured that his mode of baptism - complete immersion - is the only one that satisfies the demands of heaven, and the more rigorous members of the sect refuse communion with those who have not obeyed, as they see the command. The members of the "Christian" Church - as the disciples of Alexander Campbell term themselves - while they assent that they are tied to no creed except the New Testament, demand immersion as a prerequisite to membership in their body. The Methodist, Congregationalist, Presbyterian, Nazarene, and many others, are "evangelical" in their belief, as is a large portion of the Church of England, and its American offshoot, both of which are known as the Episcopal Church. Another portion, however, of this church is known as "ritualistic," and the two branches in England recently became so involved in a heated discussion as to the propriety of certain of their bishops partaking in official deliberations with ministers of the other, but outside, evangelistic churches, that for a time it seemed as if the whole Episcopal Church would be disrupted by the fierceness and anger gendered in the differences of opinion.

To my own mind, all this worry was much ado about nothing. Each man's brain and conscience must guide him in matters of this kind, and the worry, fret, stew, evolved out of the matter, seem to me a proof that real religion had little to do with it.

Recently one good brother came to me with tears in his voice, if not in his eyes, worried seriously as to my own religious belief because I had asserted in a public address that I believed the earnest prayer of a good Indian woman reached the ear of God as surely as did my own prayers, or those of any man, woman, minister, or priest living. To him the only effective prayers were "evangelical" prayers - whatever that may mean - and he was deeply distressed and fearfully worried because I could not see eye to eye with him in this matter. And a dear, good woman, who heard a subsequent discussion of the subject, was so worried over my attitude that she felt impelled to assure me when I left that "she would pray for me."

I have friends who are zealous Roman Catholics, and a number of them are praying that I may soon enter the folds of "Mother Church," and yet my Unitarian and Universalist friends wonder why I retain my membership in any "orthodox" church. On the other hand, my New Thought friends declare that I belong to them by the spirit of the messages I have given to the world. Then, too, my Theosophist friends - and I have many - present to me, with a force I do not attempt to controvert, the doctrine of the Universal Brotherhood of Mankind, and urge upon me acceptance of the comforting and helpful doctrine, to them, of Reincarnation.

Not long prior to this writing a good earnest man

buttonholed me and held me tight for over an hour, while he outlined his own slight divergencies from the teachings of the Methodist Church, to which he belongs, and his interpretation of the symbolism of Scripture, none of which had the slightest interest to me. In our conversation, he expressed himself as quite willing - please note the condescension - to allow me the privilege of supposing the Catholic was honest and sincere in his faith and belief, *but he really could not for one moment* allow the same to the Christian Scientist, who, from his standpoint, denied the atonement and the Divinity of Christ. I suppose if he ever picks up this booklet and reads what I am now going to write, he will regard me as a reprobate and lost beyond the possibility of salvation. Nevertheless, I wish to put on record that I regard his attitude as one of intolerance, bigotry, fanaticism, and impudence - sheer, unadulterated impertinence. Who made him the judge of the thoughts and acts of other men's inner lives? Who gave to him the wisdom and power of discernment to know that *he* was right and these others wrong? Poor, arrogant fool. His worries were not the result of genuine affection and deep human sympathy, the irrepressible and uncontrollable desires and longings of his heart to bring others into the full light of God's love, but of his overweening self-confidence in his own wisdom and judgment. And I say this in no personal condemnation of him, for I have now even forgotten who it was, but in condemnation of the spirit in which he and all his ilk ever act.

Hence, my dear reader, if you are of his class, I say to you earnestly: Don't worry about other people's salvation. It may be they are nearer saved than you are. No man can' be "worried" into accepting anything, even though *you* may deem it the only Truth. I have known men whom others regarded as agnostics who had given more study to the question of personal religion than any ten of their critics. I can recall three - all of whom were men of wonderful mentality and great earnestness of purpose. John Burroughs's first essays were written for his own soul's welfare - the results of his long-continued mental struggles for light upon the subject. Major J.W. Powell, the organizer and director for many years of the United States Geological Survey and Bureau of American Ethnology, was brought up by a father and mother whose intense longing was that their son should be a Methodist preacher. The growing youth wished to please his parents, but was also compelled to satisfy his own conscience. The more he studied the creeds and doctrines of Methodism, the less he felt he could accept them, and much to the regret of his parents, he refused to enter the ministry. Yet, in relating the story to me, he asserted that his whole life had been one long agony of earnest study to find the highest truth. Taking me into his library, where there were several extended shelves filled from end to end with the ponderous tomes of the two great government bureaus that he controlled, he said: "Most people regard this as my life-work, and outwardly it is. Yet I say to you in all sincerity that the real, inner, secret force working through all this, has been that I might satisfy my own soul on the subject of religion." Then, picking up two small volumes, he said: "In these two books I have recorded the results of my years of agonizing struggle. I don't suppose ten men have ever read them through, or, perhaps, ever will, but these are the real story of the chief work of my inner life."

I am one of the few men who have read both these books with scrupulous care, and yet were it not for what my friend told me of their profound significance to him, I should scarcely have been interested enough in their contents to read them through. At the same time, I *know* that the men who, from the standpoint of their professionally religious complacency would have condemned Major Powell, never spent one-thousandth part the time, nor felt one ten-thousandth the real solicitude that he did about seeking "the way, the truth, and the life."

Another friend in Chicago was Dr. M.H. Lackersteen, openly denounced as an agnostic, and even as an infidel, by some zealous sectaries. Yet Dr. Lackersteen had personally translated the whole of the Greek Testament, and several other sacred books of the Hebrews and Hindoos, in his intense desire to satisfy the demands of his own soul for the Truth. He was the soul of honor, the very personification of sincerity, and as much above some of his critics - whom I well knew - in these virtues, as they were above the scum of the slums.

The longer I live and study men the more I am compelled to believe that religion is a personal matter between oneself and God and is more of the spirit than most people have yet conceived. It is well known to those who have read my books and heard my lectures on the Old Franciscan Missions of California, that I revere the memory of Padres Junipero Serra, Palou, Crespi, Catala, Peyri, and others of the founders of these missions. I have equal veneration for the good-ness of many Catholic priests, nuns, and laymen of to-day. Yet I am not a Catholic, though zealous sectaries of Protestantism - even of the church to which I am supposed to belong - sometimes fiercely assail me for my open commendation of these men of that faith.

They are *worried* lest I lean too closely towards Catholicism, and ultimately become one of that fold. Others, who hear my good words in favor of what appeals to me as noble and uplifting in the lives of those of other faiths of which they do not approve, worry over and condemn my "breadth" of belief. Indeed, I have many friends who give themselves an immense lot of altogether unnecessary worry about this matter. They have labelled themselves according to some denominational tag, and accept some form of belief that, to them, seems incontrovertible and satisfactory. Many of them are praying for me, and each that I may see the TRUTH from *his* standpoint. For their prayers I am grateful. I cannot afford to lose the spirit of love behind and in every one of them. But for the *worry* about me in their minds, I have neither respect, regard, toleration, nor sympathy. I don't want it, can do without it, and I resent its being there. To each and all of them I say firmly: *Quit Your Worrying* about my religion, or want of it. I am in the hands of the same loving God that you are. I have the promise of God's Guiding Spirit as much as you have. I have listened respectfully and with an earnest and sincere desire to see and know the Truth, to all you have said, and now I want to be left alone. I have come to exclaim with Browning in *Rabbi Ben Ezra*:

Now, who shall arbitrate?
Ten men love what I hate,
Shun what I follow, slight what I receive;
Ten, who in ears and eyes
Match me. We all surmise,
They this thing, and I that: whom shall my soul believe?

For myself I have concluded that no one shall choose

my religion for me, and all the worrying in the world shall not change my attitude.

And it is to the worrying of my friends that they owe this state of mind. For this reason, I found myself one day counting up the number of people of different beliefs who had solemnly promised to pray for me. There were Methodists, Campbellites, Baptists, Roman Catholics, Episcopalians, Seventh Day Adventists, Presbyterians, Nazarenes, Holy Rollers, and others. Then the query arose: Whose prayers will be answered on my behalf? Each is sure that *his* are the ones that can be effective; yet their prayers differ; they are, to some degree, antagonistic, and insofar as they petition that I become one of their particular fold, they nullify each other, as it is utterly impossible that I accept the specific form of faith of each. The consequent result in my own mind is that as I cannot possibly become what all these good people desire I should be, as their desires and prayers for me controvert each other, I must respectfully decline to be bound by any one of them. I *must* and *will* do my own choosing. Hence all the worry on my behalf is energy, strength, and effort wasted.

Let me repeat, then, to the worrier about the salvation of others: You are in a poor business. *Quit Your Worrying.* Hands off! This is none of your concern. Believe as little or as much and what you will for your own soul's salvation, but do not put forth *your* conceptions as the *only* conceptions possible of Divine Truth before another soul who may have an immeasurably larger vision than you have. Oh, the pitiableness of man's colossal conceit, the arrogance of his ignorance. As if the God of the Universe were so small that one paltry, finite man could contain in his pint measure of a mind all the ocean of His power, knowledge, and love. Let your small and wretched worries go. Have a little larger faith in the Love of the Infinite One. Tenderly love and trust those whose welfare you seek, and trust God at the same time, but don't worry when you see the dear ones walking in a path you have not chosen for them. Remember your own ignorance, your own frailties, your own errors, your own mistakes, and then frankly and honestly, fearlessly and directly ask yourself the question if you dare to take upon your own ignorant self the responsibility of seeking to control and guide another living soul as to his eternal life.

Brother, Sister, the job is too big for you. It takes God to do that, and you are not yet even a perfect human being. Hence, while I long for all spiritual good for my sons and daughters, and for my friends, and I pray for them, it is in a large way, without any interjection of my own decisions and conclusions as to what will be good for them. I have no fears as I leave them thus in God's hand, and regard every worry as sinful on my part, and injurious to them. I have no desire that they should accept my particular brand of faith or belief. While I believe absolutely in that which I accept for the guidance of my own life, *I would not fetter their souls with my belief if I could.* They are in wiser, better, larger, more loving Hands than mine. And if I would not thus fetter my children and friends, I dare not seek to fetter others. My business is to live my own religion to the utmost. If I must worry, I will worry about that, though, as I think my readers are well aware by now, I do not believe in any kind of worry on any subject whatever.

Hence, let me again affirm in concluding this chapter, I

regard worry about the religion of others as unwarrantable on account of our own ignorances as to their peculiar needs, as well as of God's methods of supplying those needs. It is also a useless expenditure of strength, energy, and affection, for, if God leads, your worry cannot possibly affect the one so led. It is also generally an irritant to the one worried over. Even though he may not formulate it into words he feels that it is an interference with his own inner life, a nagging that he resents, and, therefore, it does him far more harm than good; and, finally, it is an altogether indefensible attempt to saddle upon another soul your own faith or belief, which may be altogether unsuitable or inadequate to the needs of that soul.

There is still one other form of worry connected with the subject of religion. Many a good man and woman worries over the apparent well-being and success of those whom he, she, accounts wicked! They are seen to flourish as a green bay tree, or as a well-watered garden, and this seems to be unfair, unjust, and unwise on the part of the powers that govern the universe. If good is desirable, people ought to be encouraged to it by material success - so reason these officially good wiseacres, who subconsciously wish to dictate to God how He should run His world.

How often we hear the question: "Why is it the wicked prosper so?" or "He's such a bad man and yet everything he does prospers." Holy Writ is very clear on this subject. The sacred writer evidently was well posted on the tendency of human nature to worry and concern itself about the affairs of others, hence his injunction:

Fret not thyself because of evil doers.

In other words, it's none of your business. And I am inclined to believe that a careful study of the Bible would reveal to every busybody who worries over the affairs of others that he himself has enough to do to attend to himself, and that his worry anyhow is a ridiculous, absurd, and senseless piece of supererogation, and rather a proof of human conceit and vanity than of true concern for the spiritual good of others.

CHAPTER XIV

AMBITION AND WORRY

Some forms of ambition are sure and certain deve-
lopers and feeders of worry and fretful distress, and
should be guarded against with jealous care. We hear a
great deal from our physicians of the germs of disease
that seize upon us and infect our whole being, but not
all the disease germs that ever infected a race are so
demoralizing to one's peace and joy as are the germs of
such deadly mental diseases as those of envy, malice,
covetousness, ambition, and the like. Ambition, like
wine, is a mocker. It is a vain deluder of men. It takes
an elevated position and beckons to you to rise, that
you may be seen and flattered of men. It does not say:
"Gain strength and power, wisdom and virtue, so that
men will place you upon the pedestal of their
veneration, respect, and love," but it bids you seize the
"spotlight" and hold it, and no sooner are you there
than it begins to pester you, as with a hundred
thousand hornets, flying around and stinging you, with
doubts and questionings as to whether your fellows see
you in this elevated place, whether they really discern
your worth, your beauty, your shining qualities; and,
furthermore, it quickens your hearing, and bids you
strain to listen to what they say about you, and as you
do so, you are pricked, stabbed, wounded by their
slighting and jeering remarks, their scornful comments

upon your impertinent and impudent arrogance at daring to take such a place, and their open denial of your possession of any of the qualities which would entitle you to so honored a position in the eyes of men.

Then, too, it must be recalled that, when fired with the desires of this mocker, ambition, one is inclined, in his selfish absorption, to be ruthless in his dealings with others. It is so easy to trample upon others when a siren is beckoning you to climb higher, and your ears are eagerly listening to her seductive phrases. With her song in your ears, you cannot hear the wails of anguish of others, upon whose rights and life you trample, the manly rebukes of those you wound, or the stern remonstrances of those who bid you heed your course. Ambition blinds and deafens, and, alas, calluses the heart, kills comradeship, drives away friendship in its eager selfishness, and in so doing, lets in a flood of worries that ever beset its victims. They may not always be in evidence while there is the momentary triumph of climbing, but they are there waiting, ready to teeter the pedestal, whisper of its unsure and unstable condition, call attention to those who are digging around its foundations, and to the fliers in the air, who threaten to hurl down bombs and completely destroy it.

Phaeton begged that his father, Phoebus Apollo, allow him to drive the flaming chariot of day through the heavens, and, in spite of all warnings and cautions, insisted upon his power and ability. Though instructed and informed as to the great dangers he evoked, he seized the reins with delight, stood up in the chariot, and urged on the snorting steeds to furious speed. Soon conscious of a lighter load than usual, the steeds dashed on, tossing the chariot as a ship at sea, and rushed headlong from the traveled road of the middle zone. The Great and Little Bear were scorched, and the Serpent that coils around the North Pole was warmed to life. Now filled with fear and dread, Phaeton lost self-control, and looked repentant to the goal which he could never reach. The unrestrained steeds dashed hither and thither among the stars, and reaching the Earth, set fire to trees, cities, harvests, mountains. The air became hot and lurid. The rivers, springs, and snowbanks were dried up. The Earth then cried out in her agony to Jupiter for relief, and he launched a thunderbolt at the now cowed and broken-hearted driver, which not only struck him from the seat he had dishonored, but also out of existence.

The old mythologists were no fools. They saw the worries, the dangers, the sure end of ambition. They wrote their cautions and warnings against it in this graphic story. Why will men and women, for the sake of an uncertain and unsure goal, tempt the Fates, and, at the same time, surely bring upon themselves a thousand unnecessary worries that sting, nag, taunt, fret, and distress? Far better seek a goal of certainty, a harbor of sureness, in the doing of kindly deeds, noble actions, unselfish devotion to the uplift of others. In this mad rush of ambitious selfishness, such a life aim may *seem* chimerical, yet it is the only aim that will reach, attain, endure. For all earthly fame, ambitious attainment, honor, glory is evanescent and temporary. Like the wealth of the miser, it must be left behind. There is no pocket in any shroud yet devised which will convey wealth across the River of Death, and no man's honors and fame but that fade in the clear light of the Spirit that shines in the land beyond.

Then, ambitious friend, quit your worrying, readjust

your aim, trim your lamp for another and better guest, live for the uplift of others, seek to give help and strength to the needy, bring sunshine to the darkened, give of your abundance of spirit and exuberance to those who have little or none, and thus will you lay up treasure within your own soul which will convert hell into heaven, and give you joy forever.

So long as men and women believe that happiness lies in outdistancing, surpassing their fellows in exterior or material things, they cannot help but be subjects to worry. To determine to gain a larger fortune than that possessed by another man is a sure invitation to worry to enter into possession of one's soul. Who has not seen the vain struggles, the distress, the worry of unsatisfied ambitions that would have amounted to nothing had they been gratified? In Women's Clubs – as well as men's - many a heart-ache is caused because some other woman gains an office, is elected to a position, is appointed on a committee you had coveted.

The remedy for this kind of worry is to change the aim of life. Instead of making position, fame, the attainment of fortune, office, a fine house, an automobile, the object of existence, make *the doing of something worthy a noble manhood or womanhood the object of your ambition.* Strive to make yourself *worthy* to be the best president your club has ever had; endeavor to be the finest equipped, mentally, for the work that is to be done, *whether you are chosen to do it or not,* and keep on, and on, and still on, finding your joy in the work, in the benefit it is to yourself, in the power it is storing up within you.

Then, as sure as the sun shines, the time will come when you will be chosen to do the needed work. "Your own will come to you." Nothing can hinder it. It will flow as certainly into your hands as the waters of the river flow into the sea.

CHAPTER XV

ENVY AND WORRY

Envy is a prolific source of worry. Once allow this demon of unrest to fasten itself in one's vitals, and worry claims every waking hour. Envy is that peculiar demon of discontent that cannot see the abilities, attainments, achievements, or possessions of another without malicious determination to belittle, deride, make light of, or absolutely deny their existence, while all the time covetously craving them for itself. Andrew Tooke pictures Envy as a vile female:

A deadly paleness in her cheek was seen;
Her meager skeleton scarce cased with skin;
Her looks awry; an everlasting scowl
Sits on her brow; her teeth deform'd and foul;
Her breast had gall more than her breast could hold;
Beneath her tongue coats of poison roll'd;
No smile e'er smooth'd her furrow'd brow but those
Which rose from laughing at another's woes;
Her eyes were strangers to the sweets of sleep,
Devouring spite for ever waking keep;
She sees bless'd men with vast success crown'd,
Their joys distract her, and their glories wound;
She kills abroad, herself's consum'd at home,
And her own crimes are her perpetual martyrdom.

Ever watching, with bloodshot eyes, the good things of others, she hates them for their possessions, longs to possess them herself, lets her covetousness gnaw hourly at her very vitals, and yet, in conversation with others, slays with slander, vile innuendo, and falsehood, the reputation of those whose virtues she covets.

As Robert Pollock wrote of one full of envy:

> It was his earnest work and daily toil
> With lying tongue, to make the noble seem
> Mean as himself.

* * * * *

> Whene'er he heard,
> As oft he did, of joy and happiness,
> And great prosperity, and rising worth,
> 'Twas like a wave of wormwood o'er his soul
> Rolling its bitterness.

Aye! and he drank in great draughts of this bitter flood, holding it in his mouth, tasting its foul and biting qualities until his whole being seemed saturated with it, hating it, dreading it, suffering every moment while doing it, yet enduring it, because of his envy at the good of others.

Few there are, who, at some time or other in their lives, do not have a taste, at least, of the stinging bite of envy. Girls are envious of each other's good looks, clothes, possessions, houses, friends; boys of the strength, skill, ability, popularity of others; women of other women, men of other men, just as when they were boys and girls.

One of the strongest words the great Socrates ever wrote was against envy. He said:

> Envy is the daughter of pride, the author of murder and revenge, the beginner of secret sedition, the perpetual tormentor of virtue. Envy is the filthy slime of the soul; a venom, a poison, a quicksilver, which consumeth the flesh, and drieth up the marrow of the bones.

And history clearly shows that the wise philosopher stated facts. Caligula slew his brother because he possessed a beauty that led him to be more esteemed and favored than he. Dionysius, the tyrant, was vindictive and cruel to Philoxenius, the musician, because he could sing; and with Plato, the philosopher, because he could dispute, better than himself. Even the great Cambyses slew his brother, Smerdis, because he was a stronger and better bowman than himself or any of his party. It was envy that led the courtiers of Spain to crave and seek the destruction of Columbus, and envy that set a score of enemies at the heels of Cortes, the conqueror of Peru.

It is a fearful and vindictive devil, is this devil of envy, and he who yields to it, who once allows it admittance to the citadel of his heart, will soon learn that every subsequent waking and even sleeping moment is one of worry and distress.

CHAPTER XVI

DISCONTENT AND WORRY

Closely allied to envy is discontent. These are blood relations, and both are prolific sources of worry. And lest there are those who think because I have revealed, in the preceding chapter, the demon of worry - envy - as one that attacks the minds of the great and mighty, it does not enter the hearts of everyday people, let me quote, entire, an article and a poem recently written by Ella Wheeler Wilcox in *The Los Angeles Examiner*. The discontent referred to clearly comes from envy. Some one has blond tresses, while she has black. This arouses her envy. She is envious because another's eyes are blue, while hers are brown; another is tall, while she is small; etc., etc. There is nothing, indeed, that she cannot weep and worry over:

There is a certain girl I know, a pretty little elf,
Who spends almost her entire thoughts in pity for herself.

Her glossy tresses, raven black, cause her to weep a pond - She is so sorry for herself because they are not blond.

Her eyes, when dry, are very bright and very brown, 'tis true, But they are almost always wet, because they are not blue.

She is of medium height, and when she sees one quite tall She weeps all day in keenest pain because she is so small.

But if she meets some tiny girl whom she considers fair, Then that she is so big herself she sobs in great despair.

When out upon a promenade her tears she cannot hide, To think she is obliged to walk while other folks can ride.

But if she drives, why then she weeps - it is so hard to be Perched stiffly in a carriage seat while other girls run free.

She used to cry herself quite sick to think she had to go Month after month to dreary schools; that was her constant woe.

But on her graduating day, my, how her tears did run! It seemed so sorrowful to know that her school life was done.

One day she wept because she saw a funeral train go by - It was so sad that she must live while other folks could die.

And really all her friends will soon join with her in those tears Unless she takes a brighter view of life ere many years.

The conceited girl or woman is tiresome and unpleasant as a companion, but the morbidly discontented woman is far worse. Perhaps you have met her, with her eternal complaint of the injustice of Fate toward her.

She feels that she is born for better things than have befallen her; her family does not understand her; her friends misjudge her; the public slights her.

If she is married she finds herself superior to her husband and to her associates. She is eternally longing for what she has not, and when she gets it is dissatisfied.

The sorrowful side of life alone appeals to her.

This she believes is due to her "artistic nature." The injustice of fortune and the unkindness of society are topics dear to her heart. She finds her only rapture in misery.

If she is religiously inclined she looks toward Heaven with more grim satisfaction in the thought that it will strip fame, favor and fortune from the unworthy than because it will give her the benefits she feels she deserves.

She does not dream that she is losing years of Heaven here upon earth by her own mental attitude.

WE BUILD OUR HEAVENS THOUGHT BY THOUGHT.

If you are dwelling upon the dark phases of your destiny and upon the ungracious acts of Fate, you are shaping more of the same experience for yourself here and in realms beyond.

You are making happiness impossible for yourself upon any plane. In your own self lies Destiny.

I have known a woman to keep her entire family despondent for years by her continual assertions that she was out of her sphere, misunderstood and unappreciated.

The minds of sensitive children accepted these statements and grieved over "Poor Mother's" sad life until their own youth was embittered. The morbid mother seized upon the sympathies of her children like a leech and sapped their young lives of joy.

The husband grew discouraged and indifferent under the continual strain, and what might have been a happy home was a desolate one, and its memory is a nightmare to the children to-day.

Understand yourself and your Divine possibilities and you will cease to think you are misunderstood.

It is not possible to misunderstand a beautiful, sunny day. All nature rejoices in its loveliness.

Give love, cheerfulness, kindness and good-will to all humanity, and you need not worry about being misunderstood.

Give the best you have to each object, purpose and individual, and you will eventually receive the best from humanity.

CHAPTER XVII

COWARDICE AND WORRY

Cowardice is a much more prolific source of worry than most people imagine. There are many varieties of cowardice, all tracing their ancestry back to fear. Fear truly makes cowards of us all. There are the physical cowards, the social cowards, the business cowards, the hang-on-to-your-job cowards, the political cowards, the moral cowards, the religious cowards, and fifty-seven, nay, a hundred and one other varieties. Each and all of these have their own attendant demons of worry. Every barking dog becomes a lion ready to tear one to pieces, and no bridge is strong enough to allow us to pass over in safety. No cloud has a silver lining, and every rain-storm is sure to work injury to the crops rather than bring the needful moisture for their vivification.

What a piteous sight to see a man who dares not express his honest opinions, who must crawl instead of walk upright, in the presence of his employer, lest he lose his job. How his cowardice worries him, meets him at every turn, torments him, lest some incautious word be repeated, lest he say or do the wrong thing. And so long as there are cowards to employ, bully employers will exist. Nay, the cowardice seems to call out bullying qualities. Just as a cur will follow you with barkings and threatening growls if you run from him, and yet turn tail and run when you boldly face him, so with most men, with society, with the world - flee from them, show your fear of them, and they will harry you, but boldly face them, they gentle down immediately, fawn upon you, lie down, or, to use an expressive slang phrase, "come and eat out of your hand."

How politicians straddle the fence, refrain from expressing their opinions, deal in glittering generalities, because of their cowardly fears. How they turn their sails to catch every breath of popular favor. How cautious, politic, wary, they are, and how fears worry and besiege them, whenever they accidentally or incidentally say something that can be interpreted as a positive conviction. And yet men really love a brave man in political life; one who has definite convictions and fearlessly states them; who has no worries as to results but dares to say and do those things only of which his conscience approves. No matter how one may regard Roosevelt, cowardice is one thing none will accuse him of. He says his say, does his will, expresses himself with freedom upon any and all subjects, let results be as they may. Such a man is free from the petty worries that beset most politicians. He knows nothing of their existence. They cannot breathe in the free atmosphere that is essential to his life; like the cowardly cur, they run away at his approach.

Oh, cowards all, of every kind and degree, quit ye like men, be strong and of good courage, dare and do, dare and say, dare and be, take a manly stand, fling out your banner boldly to the breeze, cry out as did Patrick Henry: "Give me liberty, or give me death," or as that other patriot did: "Sink or swim, survive or perish, I give my hand and my heart to this vote." Do the things you are afraid of; dare the men who make cowards of you; say the things you fear to say; and be the things you know you ought to be, and it will surprise you how the petty devils of worry will slink away from you. You will walk in new life, in new strength, in new joy, in new freedom. For he who lives a life free from worries of this nature, has a spontaneity, a freedom, an exuberance, an enthusiasm, a boldness, that not only are winsome in themselves, make friends, open the doors of opportunity, attract the moving elements of life, but that give to their possessor an entirely new outlook, a wider survey, a more comprehensive grasp. Life itself becomes bigger, grander, more majestic, more worth while, the whole horizon expands, and from being a creature of petty affairs, dabbling in a small way in the stuff of which events are made, he becomes a potent factor, a man, a creator, a god, though in the germ.

CHAPTER XVIII

WORRY ABOUT MANNERS AND SPEECH

Many people are desperately worried about their manners. One has but to read the letters written to the "Answers to Correspondents" departments of the newspapers to see how much worry this subject of manners causes. This springs, undoubtedly, from a variety of causes. People brought up in the country, removing to the city, find the conditions of life very different from those to which they have been accustomed, and they are *uncertain* as to what city people regard as the right and proper things to do. Where one, perforce, must act, uncertainty is always irritating or worrying, and, because of this uncertainty, many people worry even before the time comes to act. Now, if their worry would take a practical and useful turn - or, perhaps, I had better state it in another way, viz., that if they would spend the same time in deciding what their course of action should be - there would be an end put to the worry.

We have all seen such people. They are worried lest their clothes are not all right for the occasion, lest their tie is of the wrong shade, their shoes of the correct style, and a thousand and one things that they seem to conjure up for the especial purpose of worrying over them. Who has not seen the nervousness, the worried expression on the face, the real misery of such people, caused by trifles that are so insignificant as not to be worth one-tenth the bother wasted on them.

The learning of a few fundamental principles will help out wonderfully. The chief end of "good manners" is to oil the wheels of social converse. Hence, the first and most important principle to learn is a due and proper consideration for the rights, opinions, and comfort of others. In other words, don't think of yourself so much as of the other fellow. Let your question be, not: How can I secure my own pleasure and comfort? but How can I best secure his? It is a self-evident proposition that you cannot make him feel comfortable and happy if you are uncomfortable and unhappy. Hence, the first thing to do is to quit worrying and be comfortable. This desired state of mind will come as soon as you have courageously made up your mind as to what standard of manners you intend to follow. The world is made up to-day, largely, of two classes: those who have money, and those who don't. Of the former class, a certain few set themselves up as the arbiters of good manners; they decide what shall be called "good form," and what is not allowable. If you belong to that class, the best thing you can do is to learn "to play the game their way." Study their rules of calling cards, and learn whether you leave one, two, three, or six when you are calling upon a man, or a woman, or both, or their oldest unmarried daughter, or the rest of the family. This is a regular game like golf, or polo. You have to know the course, the tools to use, and the method of going from one goal to another. Now, I never knew any ordinarily intelligent man or woman who couldn't learn the names of the tools used in golf, the numbers of the holes, and the rules of the game. *How* you play the game is another matter. And so is it in "good society." You can learn the rules as easily as the next one, and then it is "up to you" as to *how* you play it. You'll have to study the fashions in clothes; the fashions in handkerchiefs, and how to flirt with them; when to drink tea, and where; how to lose money gracefully at bridge; how to gabble incessantly and not know what you are talking about; how to listen "intelligently" and not have the remotest idea what your *vis-a-vis* is saying to you; you'll have to join 'steen clubs, and read ten new novels a day; go to every new play; know all about the latest movies; know all the latest ideas of social uplift, study art, the spiritual essence of color, the futurists, and the cubists. Of course, you'll study the peerage of England and know all about rank and precedence - and, indeed, you'll have your hands and mind so full of things that will make such a hash of life that it will take ten specialists to straighten you out and help you to die forty years before your time. Hence, if that is the life you intend to live, throw this book into the fire. It will be wasting your time to read it.

If you don't belong to the class of the extra rich, but are all the time wishing that you did; that you had their money, could live as they live, and, as far as you can, you imitate, copy, and follow them, then, again, I recommend that you give this book to the nearest newsboy and let him sell it and get some good out of it. You are not yet ready for it, or else you have gone so far beyond me in life, that you are out of my reach.

If, on the other hand, you belong to the class of *workers*, those who have to earn their living and wish to spend their lives intelligently and usefully, you can well afford to disregard - after you have learned to apply the few basic principles of social converse - the whims, the caprices, the artificial code set up by the so-called arbiters of fashion, manners, and "good form," which are not formulated for the promotion of intelligent intercourse between real manhood and womanhood, but for the preservation and strengthening of the barriers of wealth and caste.

Connected with this phase of the subject is a consideration of those who are worried lest in word or action, they fail in gentility. They are afraid to do anything lest it should not be regarded as genteel. When they shake hands, it must be done not so much with hearty, friendly spontaneity, but with gentility, and you wonder what that faint touch of fingers, reached high in air, means. They would be mortified beyond measure if they failed to observe any of the little gentilities of life, while the larger consideration of their visitor's disregard of the matter, would entirely escape them. To such people, social intercourse is a perpetual worry and bugbear. They are on the watch every moment, and if a visitor fails to say, "Pardon me," at the proper place, or stands with his back to his hostess for a moment, or does any other of the things that natural men and women often do, they are "shocked."

Then it would be amusing, were it not pathetic, to see how particular they are about their speech - *what* they say, and *how* they say it. As Dr. Palmer has tersely said: "We are terrorized by custom, and inclined to adjust what we would say to what others have said before," and he might have added: It must be said in the same manner.

I cannot help asking why men and women should be terrorized by custom - the method followed or prescribed by other men and women. Why be so afraid of others; why so anxious to "kow-tow" to the standards of others? Who are they? What are they, that they should demand the reverent following of the world? Have you anything to say? Have you a right to say it? Is it wise to say it? Then, in the name of God, of manhood, of common sense, say it, directly, positively, assertively, as is your right, remembering the assurance of the Declaration of Independence that "all men are created equal." Don't worry about whether you are saying it in the genteel fashion of some one else's standard. Make your own standard. Even the standards of the grammar books and dictionaries are not equal to that of a man who has something to say and says it forcefully, truthfully, pointedly, directly. Dr. Palmer has a few words to say on this phase of the subject, which are well worthy serious consideration: "The cure for the first of these troubles is to keep our eyes on our object, instead of on our listener or ourselves; and for the second, to learn to rate the expressiveness of language more highly than its compeers. The opposite of this, the disposition to set correctness above expressiveness, produces that peculiarly vulgar diction, known as "school-ma'am English," in which for the sake of a dull accord with usage, all the picturesque, imaginative, and forceful employment of words is sacrificed."

There you have it! If you have something to say that really means something, think of that, rather than of the way of saying it, your hearer, or yourself. Thus you will lose your self-consciousness, your dread, your fear, your worry. If your thought is worth anything, you can afford to laugh at some small violation of grammar, or the knocking over of some finical standard or other. Not that I would be thought to advocate either carelessness, laziness, or indifference in speech. Quite the contrary, as all who have heard me speak well know. But I fully believe that *thought* is of greater importance than *form of expression*. And, as for grammar, I believe with Thomas Jefferson, that "whenever, by small grammatical negligences, the energy of your ideas can be condensed or a word be made to stand for a sentence, I hold grammatical rigor in contempt."

I was present once when Thomas Carlyle and a technical grammarian were talking over some violation of correct speech - according to the latter's standard - when Carlyle suddenly burst forth in effect, in his rich Scotch burr: "Why, mon, I'd have ye ken that I'm one of the men that make the language for little puppies like ye to paw over with your little, fiddling, twiddling grammars!"

By all means, know all the grammar you can. Read the best of poets and prose authors to see how they have mastered the language, but don't allow your life to become a burden to you and others because of your worry lest you "slip a grammatical cog" here and there, when you know you have something worth saying. And if you haven't anything worth saying, please, please, keep your mouth shut, no matter what the genteel books prescribe, for nothing can justify the talk of an empty-headed fool who will insist upon talking when he and his listeners know he has nothing whatever to say. So, if you must worry, let it be about something worth while - getting hold of ideas, the strength of your thought, the power of your emotion, the irresistible sweep of your enthusiasm, the force-fulness of your indignation about wrong. These are things it is worth while to set your mind upon, and when you have decided what you ought to say, and are absorbed with the power of its thought, the need the world has for it, you will care little about the exact form of your words. Like the flood of a mighty stream, they will pour forth, carrying conviction with them, and to convince your hearer of some powerful truth is an object worthy the highest endeavor of a godlike man or woman - surely a far different object than worrying as to whether the words or method of expression meet some absurd standard of what is conceived to be "gentility."

Congressman Hobson, of Merrimac fame, and Ex-President Roosevelt are both wonderful illustrations of the point I am endeavoring to impress upon my readers. I heard Hobson when, in Philadelphia, at a public dinner given in his honor, he made his first speech after his return from Cuba. It was evident that he had been, and was, much worried about what he should say, and the result was everybody else was worried as he tried to say it. His address was a pitiable failure, mainly because he had little or nothing to say, and yet tried to make a speech. Later he entered Congress, began to feel intensely upon the subjects of national defense and prohibition of the alcoholic liquor traffic. A year or so ago I heard him speak on the latter of these subjects. Here, now, was an entirely different man. He was possessed with a great idea. He was no longer trying to find something to say, but in a power-ful, earnest, and enthusiastic way, he poured forth facts, figures, argument, and illustration, that could not fail to convince an open mind, and profoundly impress even the prejudiced.

It was the same with Roosevelt. When he first began to speak in public, it was hard work. He wrote his addresses beforehand, and then read them. Perhaps he does now, for aught I know to the contrary, but I do know that now that he is full of the subjects of national honor in dealing with such cases as Mexico, Belgium, and Armenia, and our preparedness to sacrifice life itself rather than honor, his words pour forth in a perfect Niagara of strong, robust, manly argument, protest, and remonstrance, which gives one food for deep thought no matter how much he may differ.

There are those who worry about the "gentility" of others. I remember when Charles Wagner, the author of *The Simple Life*, was in this country. We were dining at the home of a friend and one of these super-sensitive, finical sticklers for gentility was present. Wagner was speaking in his big, these super-sensitive, finical sticklers for gentility simple, primitive way of a man brought up as a peasant, and more concerned about what he was thinking than whether his "table manners" conformed to the latest standard. There was some gravy on his plate. He wanted it. He took a piece of bread and used it as a sop, and then, impaling the gravy-soaked bread on his fork, he conveyed it to his mouth with gusto and relish. My "genteel" friend commented upon it afterwards as "disgusting," and lost all interest in the man and his work as a consequence.

To my mind, the criticism was that of a fool.

John Muir, the eminent poet-naturalist of the *Mountains of California*, had a habit at the table of "crumming" his bread - that is, toying with it, until it crumbled to pieces in his hand. He would, at the same time, be sending out a steady stream of the most entertaining, interesting, fascinating, and instructive lore about birds and beasts, trees and flowers, glaciers and rocks, that one ever listened to. In his mental occupancy, he knew not whether he was eating his soup with a fork or an ice-cream spoon - and cares less. Neither did any one else with brains and an awakened mind that soared above mere conventional manners. And yet I once had an Eastern woman of great wealth, (recently acquired), and of great pretensions to social "manners," at whose table Muir had eaten, inform me that she regarded him as a rude boor, because, forsooth, he was unmindful of these trivial and unimportant conventions when engaged in conversation.

Now, neither Wagner nor Muir would justify any advocacy on my part of neglect of true consideration, courtesy, or good manners. But where is the "lack of breeding" in sopping up gravy with a piece of bread or "crumming," or eating soup with a spoon of one shape or another? These are purely arbitrary rules, laid down by people who have more time than sense, money than brains, and who, as I have elsewhere remarked, are far more anxious to preserve the barand unimportant conventions when engaged in conive realization of the biblical idea of the "brotherhood of man."

CHAPTER XIX

THE WORRIES OF JEALOUSY

A prolific source of worry is jealousy; not only the jealousy that exists between men and women, but that exists between women and women, and between men and men. There are a thousand forms that this hideous monster of evil assumes, and when they have been catalogued and classified, another thousand will be found awaiting, around the corner, of entirely different categories. But all alike they have one definite origin, one source, one cause. And that cause, I am convinced, is selfishness. We wish to own, to dominate, to control, absolutely, entirely, for our own pleasure, and satisfaction, that of which we are jealous. In Chapter One I tell the incident of the young man on the street car whose jealous worry was so manifest when he saw his "girl" smiling upon another man. I suppose most men and women feel, or have felt, at some time or other, this sex jealousy. That woman belongs to *me*, her smiles are *mine*, her pleasant words should fall on *my* ear alone; *I* am her lover, she, the mistress of *my* heart; and that should content her.

Every writer of the human heart has expatiated upon this great source of worry - jealousy. Shakspere refers to it again and again. The whole play of *Othello* rests upon the Moor's jealousy of his fair, sweet, and loyally

faithful Desdemona. How the fiendish Iago plays upon
Othello's jealous heart until one sees that:

> Trifles, light as air,
> Are to the jealous confirmations strong
> As proofs of holy writ.

Iago bitterly resents a slight he feels Othello has put
upon him. With his large, generous, unsuspicious
nature, Othello never dreams of such a thing; he trusts
Iago as his intimate friend, and thus gives the crafty
fiend the oportunity he desires to

> put the Moor
> Into a jealousy so strong
> That judgment cannot cure ...
> Make the Moor thank me, love me, reward me,
> For making him egregiously an ass
> And practicing upon his peace and quiet
> Even to madness.

Othello gives his wife, Desdemona, a rare handkerchief. Iago urges his own wife, who is Desdemona's
maid, to pilfer this and bring it to him. When he gets it,
he leaves it in Cassio's room. Cassio was an intimate
friend of Othello's, one, indeed, who had gone with
him when he went to woo Desdemona, and who, by
Iago's machinations, had been suspended from his
office of Othello's chief lieutenant. To provoke
Othello's jealousy Iago now urges Desdemona to plead
Cassio's cause with her husband, and at the came time
eggs on Othello to watch Cassio:

> Look to your wife; observe her well with Cassio;
> Wear your eye thus, not jealous nor secure.
> I would not have your free and noble nature

Out of self-bounty be abus'd; look to 't.

Thus he works Othello up to a rage, and yet all the time pretends to be holding him back:

I do see you're mov'd;
I pray you not to strain my speech
To grosser issues nor to larger reach
Than to suspicion.

Iago leaves the handkerchief in Cassio's room, at the same time saying:

The Moor already changes with my poison;
Dangerous conceits are in their natures poisons,
Which at the first are scarce found to distaste,
But with a little act upon the blood,
Burn like the mines of sulphur.

And as he sees the tortures the jealous worries of the Moor have already produced in him, he exultingly yet stealthily rejoices:

Not poppy, nor mandragora,
Nor all the drowsy syrups of the world,
Shall ever medicine thee to that sweet sleep
Which thou hadst yesterday.

Well might Othello exclaim that he is "Set on the rack." Each new suspicion is a fresh pull of the lever, a tightening of the strain to breaking point, and soon his jealousy turns to the fierce and murderous anger Iago hoped it would:

Like to the Pontic sea,
Whose icy current and compulsive course

Ne'er feels retiring ebb, but keeps due on
To the Propontic and the Hellespont,
Even so my bloody thoughts, with violent pace,
Shall ne'er look back, ne'er ebb to humble love,
Till that a capable and wide revenge
Swallow them up.

Thus was he urged on, worried by his jealousy, until, in his bloody rage, he slew his faithful wife. Poor Desdemona, we weep her fate, yet at the same time we should deeply lament that Othello was so beguiled and seduced by his jealousy to so horrible a deed. And few men or women there are, unless their souls are purified by the wisdom of God, that are not liable to jealous influences. Our human nature is weak and full of subtle treacheries, that, like Iago, seduce us to our own undoing. He who yields for one moment to the worries of jealousy is already on the downward path that leads to misery, woe and deep undoing, Iago is made to declare the philosophy of this fact, when, in the early portion of the play he says to Roderigo:

'Tis in ourselves we are thus or thus. Our bodies are our gardens, to the which our wills are gardeners; so that if we will plant nettles or sow lettuce, set hyssop and weed up thyme, supply it with one gender of herbs or distract it with many, either to have it sterile with idleness or manured with industry, why, the power and corrigible authority of this lies in our wills.

Therein, surely, is great truth. We can plant or weed up, in the garden of our minds, whatever we will; we can "have it sterile with idleness," or fertilize it with industry, and it must ever be remembered that the more fertile the soil the more evil weeds will grow apace if we water and tend them. Our jealous worries are the poisonous weeds of life's garden and should be rooted out instanter, and kept out, until not a sign of them can again be found.

Solomon sang that "jealousy is as cruel as the grave; the coals thereof are coals of fire, which hath a most vehement flame."

What a graphic picture of worry - a fire of vehement flame, burning, scorching, destroying peace, happiness, content, joy and reducing them to ashes.

In my travel and observation I have found a vast amount of jealous worry in institutions of one kind and another - such as the Indian Service, in reform schools, in humane societies, in hospitals, among the nurses, etc. It seems to be one of the misfortunes of weak human nature when men and women associate themselves together to do some work which ought to call out all the nobleness, the magnanimity, the godlike qualities of their souls, they become maggoty with jealous worries - worry that they are not accorded the honor that is their due; worry that *their* work is not properly appreciated; worry lest someone else becomes a favorite of the Superintendent, etc., etc., etc., *ad libitum*. Worries of this nature in every case, are a proof of small, or undeveloped, natures. No truly great man or woman can be jealous. Jealousy implies that you are not sure of your own worth, ability, power. You find someone else is being appreciated, you *covet* that appreciation for yourself, whether you deserve it or not. In other words you yield to accursed selfishness, utterly forgetful of the apostolic injunction: "In honor preferring one another."

And the same jealousies are found among men and women in every walk of life, in trade, in the office, among professors in schools, colleges, universities; in the learned professions, among lawyers, physicians and even among the ministers of the gospel, and judges upon the bench.

Oh! shame! shame! upon the littleness, the meanness, the paltriness of such jealousies; of the worries that come from them. How any human being is to be pitied whose mortal mind is corroded with the biting acid of jealous worry. When I see those who are full of worry because yielding to this demon of jealousy I am almost inclined to believe in the old-time Presbyterian doctrine of "total depravity." Whenever, where-ever, you find yourself feeling jealous, take yourself by the throat (figuratively), and strangle the feeling, then go and frankly congratulate the person of whom you are jealous upon some good you can truthfully say you see in him; spread his praises abroad; seek to do him honor. Thus by active work against your own paltry emotion you will soon overcome it and be free from its damning and damnable worries.

Akin to the worries of jealousy are the worries of hate. How much worry hate causes the hater, he alone can tell. He spends hours in conjuring up more reasons for his hate than he would care to write down. Every success of the hated is another stimulant to worry, and each step forward is a sting full of pain and bitterness.

He who hates walks along the path of worry, and so long as he hates he must worry. Hence, there is but one practical way of escape from the worries of hatred, viz., by ceasing to hate, by overcoming evil with good.

CHAPTER XX

THE WORRIES OF SUSPICION

He who has a suspicious mind is ever the prey of worry. Such an one is to be pitied for he is tossed hither and yon, to and fro, at the whim of every breath of suspicion he breathes. He has no real peace of mind, no content, no unalloyed joy, for even in his hours of pleasure, of recreation, of expected jollity he is worrying lest someone is trying to get ahead of him, his *vis-a-vis* is "jollying" him, his partner at golf is trying to steal a march on him, he is not being properly served at the picnic, etc.

These suspicious-minded people are sure that every man is a scoundrel at heart - more or less - and needs to be watched; no man or woman is to be trusted; every grocer will sand his sugar, chicory his coffee, sell butterine for butter, and cold-storage eggs for fresh if he gets a chance. To accept the word of a stranger is absurd, as it is also to believe in the disinterestedness of a politician, reformer, office-holder, a corporation, or a rich man. But to believe evil, to expect to be swindled, or prepare to be deceived is the height of perspicacity and wisdom. How wonderfully Shakspere in *Othello* portrays the wretchedness of the suspicious man. One reason why Iago so hated the Moor was that he suspected him:

the thoughts whereof
Doth like a poisonous mineral gnaw my inwards,
And nothing can or shall content my soul
Till I am even'd with him.

How graphic the simile, "gnaw my inwards;" it is the
perpetual symbol of worry; the poisonous mineral ever
biting away the lining of the stomach; just as mice and
rats gnaw at the backs of the most precious books and
destroy them; aye, as they gnaw during the night-time
and drive sleep away from the weary, so does
suspicion gnaw with its sharp worrying teeth to the
destruction of peace, happiness and joy.

Then, when Iago has poisoned Othello's mind with
suspicions about his wife, how the Moor is worried,
gnawed by them:

By heaven, he echoes me,
As if there were some monster in his thought
Too hideous to be shown - (To Iago) Thou dost
mean something.
I heard thee say even now, thou lik'dst not that,
When Cassio left my wife; what didst not like?
And when I told thee he was of my counsel
In my whole course of wooing, thou criedst
'Indeed!'
And didst contract and purse thy brow together,
As if thou then hadst shut up in thy brain
Some horrible conceit. If thou dost love me,
Show me thy thought.

And then we know, how, with crafty, devilish cunning,
Iago plays upon these suspicions, fans their spark into
flames. He pretends to be doing it purely on Othello's
account and accuses himself that:

> it is my nature's plague
> To spy into abuses, and yet my jealousy
> Shapes faults that are not:

and then cries out:

> O beware, my lord, of jealousy!
> It is the green-eyed monster which doth mock
> The meat it feeds on. That cuckold lives in bliss
> Who certain of his fate, loves not his wronger;
> But, O, what damned minutes tells he o'er
> Who dotes, yet doubts, suspects, yet strongly loves!

There, indeed, the woe of the suspicious is shown. His minutes are really "damned;" peace flies his heart, rest from his couch, sanity from his throne, and, *yielding* himself, he becomes filled with murderous anger and imperils his salvation here and hereafter.

CHAPTER XXI

THE WORRIES OF IMPATIENCE

How many of our worries come from impatience? We do not want to wait until the fruition of our endeavors comes naturally, until the time is ripe, until we are ready for that which we desire. We wish to overrule conditions which are beyond our power; we fail to accept the inevitable with a good grace; we refuse to believe in our circumscriptions, our limitations, and in our arrogance and pride express our anger, our indignation, our impatience.

I have seen people whose auto has broken down, worried fearfully because they would not arrive somewhere as they planned, and in their impatient fretfulness they annoyed, angered, and upset all around them, without, in one single degree, improving their own condition or hastening the repair of the disaster. What folly; what more than childish foolishness.

A child may be excused for its impatience and petulance for it has not yet learned the inevitable facts of life - such as that breaks must be repaired, tires must be made so that they will not leak, and that the gasoline tank cannot be empty if the machine is to run. But a man, a woman, is supposed to have learned these incontrovertible facts, and should, at the same time, have learned acquiesence in them.

A train is delayed; one has an important engagement; worry seems inevitable and excusable. But is it? Where is the use? Will it replace the destroyed bridge, renew the washed out track, repair the broken engine? How much better to submit to the inevitable with graceful acceptance of the fact, than to fret, stew, worry, and at the same time, irritate everyone around you.

How serenely Nature rebukes the impatience of the fretful worrier. A man plants corn, wheat, barley, potatoes - or trees, that take five, seven years to come to bearing, such as the orange, olive, walnut, date, etc. Let him fret ever so much, worry all he likes, chafe and fret every hour; let him go and dig up his seeds or plants to urge their upgrowing; let him even swear in his impatient worry and threaten to smash all his machinery, discharge his men, and turn his stock loose; Nature goes on her way, quietly, unmoved, serenely, unhurried, undisturbed by the folly of the one creature of earth who is so senseless as to worry - viz., man.

Many a man's hair has turned gray, and many a woman's brow and cheeks have become furrowed because of fretful, impatient worry over something that could not be changed, or hastened, or improved.

My conception of life is that manhood, womanhood, should rise superior to any and all conditions and circumstances. Whatever happens, Spirit should be supreme, superior, in control. And until we learn that lesson, life, so far, has failed. Inasmuch as we do learn it, life has become a success.

CHAPTER XXII

THE WORRIES OF ANTICIPATION

He crosses every bridge before he comes to it, is a graphic and proverbial rendering of a description of the man who worries in anticipation. Something, sure, is going to happen. He is always fearful, not of what is, but of what is going to be. For twenty years he has managed to live and pay his rent, but at the beginning of each month he begins afresh to worry where "next month's rent is going to come from." He's collected his bills fairly well for a business life-time, but if a debtor fails to send in his check on the very day he begins to worry and fear lest he fail to receive it. His wife has given him four children, but at the coming of the fifth he is sure something extraordinarily painful and adverse is going to happen.

He sees - possibly, here, I should say, *she* sees - their son climbing a tree. She is sure he will fall and break a leg, an arm, or his neck. Her boy mustn't ride the horse lest he fall and injure himself; if he goes to swim he is surely in danger of being drowned, and she could never allow him or his sister to row in a boat lest it be overturned. The child must be watched momentarily, lest it fall out of the window, search out a sharp knife, swallow poison, or do some irreparable damage to the bric-a-brac.

Here let me relate an incident the truth of which is vouched for, and which clearly illustrates the difference between the attitude of worry and that of trust. One day, when Flattich, a pious minister of the Wurtemberg, was seated in his armchair, one of his foster children fell out of a second-story window, right before him, to the pavement below. He calmly ordered his daughter to go and bring up the child. On doing so it was found the little one had sustained no injury. A neighbor, however, aroused by the noise, came in and reproached Flattich for his carelessness and inattention. While she was thus remonstrating, her own child, which she had brought with her, fell from the bench upon which she had seated it, and broke its arm. "Do you see, good woman," said the minister, "if you imagine yourself to be the sole guardian of your child, then you must constantly carry it in your arms. I commend my children to God; and even though they then fall, they are safer than were I to devote my whole time and attention to them."

Those who anticipate evils for their children too often seem to bring down upon their loved ones the very evils they are afraid of. And one of the greatest lessons of life, and one that brings immeasurable and uncountable joys when learned, is, that Nature - the great Father-Mother of us all - is kindly disposed to us. We need not be so alarmed, so fearful, so anticipatory of evil at her hands.

Charles Warren Stoddard used to tell of the great dread Mark Twain was wont to feel, during the exhaustion and reaction he felt at the close of each of his lectures, lest he should become incapable of further writing and lecturing and therefore become dependent upon his friends and die a pauper. How wonderfully he conquered this demon of perpetual worry all those who know his life are aware; how that, when his publisher failed he took upon himself a heavy financial burden, for which he was in no way responsible, went on a lecture tour around the world and paid every cent of it, and finally died with his finances in a most prosperous condition.

The anticipatory worries of others are just as senseless, foolish and absurd as were those of Mark Twain, and it is possible for every man to overcome them, even as did he.

The cloud we anticipate seldom, if ever, comes, and then, generally, in a different direction from where we sought it. Time spent on looking for the cloud, and figuring how much of injury it will do us had better be utilized in garnering the hay crop, bringing in the lambs, or hauling warm fodder and bedding for them.

There is another side, however, to this worrying anticipation of troubles. The ancient philosophers recognized it. Lucan wrote: "The very fear of approaching evil has driven many into peril."

There are those who believe that the very concentration of thought upon a possible evil will bring to pass the peculiar arrangement of circumstances that makes the evil. Of this belief I am not competent to speak, but I am fully assured that it is far from helpful to be contemplating the possibility of evil. In my own life I have found that worrying over evils in anticipation has not prevented their coming, and, on the other hand, that where I have boldly faced the situation, without fear and its attendant worries, the evil has fled.

Hence, whether worries in hand, or worries to come, worries real or worries imaginary, the wise, sane and practical course is to kill them all and thus *Quit Your Worrying*.

CHAPTER XXIII

HOW OUR WORRY AFFECTS OTHERS

If worry affected merely ourselves it would be bad enough, but we could tolerate it more than we do. For it is one of the infernal characteristics of worry that our manifestation of it invariably affects others as injuriously as it affects ourselves.

An employer who worries his employees never gets the good work out of them as does the one who has sense enough to keep them happy, good-natured and contented. I was lecturing once for a large corporation. I had two colleagues, who "spelled me" every hour. For much of the time we had no place to rest, work or play between our lectures. Our engagement lasted the better part of a year, and the result was that, during that period where our reasonable needs were unprovided for, we all failed to give as good work as we were capable of. We were unnecessarily worried by inadequate provision and our employers suffered. Henry Ford, and men of his type have learned this lesson. Men respond rapidly to those who do not worry them. Governor Hunt and Warden Sims, of Arizona, have learned the same fact in dealing with prisoners of the State Penitentiary. The less the men are "worried" by unnecessarily harsh treatment, absurd and cruel restrictions, curtailment of natural rights, the better they act, the easier they are liable to reform and make good.

Dr. Musgrove to his *Nervous Breakdowns*, tells a story of two commanders which well illustrates this point:

> In a certain war two companies of men had to march an equal distance in order to meet at a particular spot. The one arrived in perfect order, and with few signs of exhaustion, although the march had been an arduous one. The other company reached the place utterly done up and disorganised. It was all a question of leadership; the captain of the first company had known his way and kept his men in good order, while the captain of the second company had never been sure of himself, and had harassed his subordinates with a constant succession of orders and counter-orders, until they had hardly known whether they were on their heads or their heels. That was why they arrived completely demoralised.

In war, as in peace, it is not work that kills so much as worry. A general may make his soldiers work to the point of exhaustion as Napoleon often did, yet have their almost adoring worship. But the general who worries his men gets neither their good will nor good work.

A worrying mother can keep a whole house in a turmoil, from father down to the latest baby. The growing boys and girls soon learn to dread the name of "home," and would rather be in school, in the backyard playing, in the attic, at the neighbors, or in the streets, anywhere, than within the sound of their mother's worrying voice, or frowning countenance. A worrying husband can drive his wife distracted, and vice versa. I was dining not long ago with a couple that, from outward appearance, had everything that heart could desire to make them happy. They were young, healthy, had a good income, were *both* engaged in work they liked, yet the husband worried the wife constantly about trifles. If she wished to set the table in a particular way he worried because she didn't do it some other way; if she drove one of their autos he worried because she didn't take the other; and when she wore a spring-day flowery kind of a hat he worried her because his mother never wore any other than a black hat. The poor woman was distracted by the absolute absurdities, frivolities and inconsequentialities of his worries, yet he didn't seem to have sense to see what he was doing. So I gave him a plain practical talk - as I had been drawn into a discussion of the matter without any volition on my part - and urged him to quit irritating his wife so foolishly and so unnecessarily.

Some teachers worry their pupils until the latter fail to do the work they are competent to do; and the want of success of many an ambitious teacher can often be attributed to his, her, worrying disposition. Remember, therefore, that when you worry you are making others unhappy as well as yourself, you are putting a damper, a blight, upon other lives as well as your own, you are destroying the efficiency of other workers as well as your own, you are robbing others of the joy of life which God intended them freely to possess. So that for the sake of others, as well as your own, it becomes an imperative duty that you

QUIT YOUR WORRYING.

CHAPTER XXIV

WORRY VERSUS INDIFFERENCE

The aim and object of all striving in life should be to grow more human, more humane, less selfish, more helpful to our fellows. Any system of life that fails to meet this universal need is predestined to failure. When, therefore, I urge upon my readers that they quit their worrying about their husbands or wives, sons and daughters, neighbors and friends, the wicked and the good, I do not mean that they are to harden their hearts and become indifferent to their welfare. God forbid! No student of the human heart, of human life, and of the Bible can long ignore the need of a caution upon these lines. The sacred writer knew what he was talking about when he spoke of the human heart as deceitful and desperately wicked. It is deceitful or it would never blind people as it does to the inutility, the futility of much of their goodness. A goodness that is wrapped up in a napkin, and lies unused for the benefit of others, rots and becomes a putrid mass of corrupttion. It can only remain good by being unselfishly used for the good of others, and to prove that the human heart is desperately wicked one needs only to look at the suffering endured by mankind unnecessarily - suffering that organized society ought to prevent and render impossible.

The parable of the lost sheep was written to give us this needful lesson. The shepherd, when he found one of his sheep gone, did not sit down and wring his hands in foolish and useless worry as to what would happen to the sheep, the dangers that would beset it, the thorns, the precipices, the wolves. Nor did he count over the times he had cautioned the sheep not to get away from its fellows. Granted that it was conceited, self-willed, refused to listen to counsel, disobedient - the main fact in the mind of the shepherd was that it was lost, unprotected, in danger, afraid, cold, hungry, longing for the sheepfold, the companionship of its fellows and the guardianship of the shepherd. Hence, he went out eagerly and sympathetically, and searched until he found it and brought it back to shelter.

This, then, should be the spirit of those who have needed my caution and advice to quit their worrying about their loved ones and others - Do not worry, but do not, under any consideration, become hard-hearted, careless, or indifferent. Better by far preserve your interest and the human tenderness that leads you to the useless and needless expenditure of energy and sympathy in worry than that you should let your loved ones suffer without any care, thought, or endeavor on their behalf. But do not let it be a sympathy that leads to worry. Let it be helpful, stimulating, directive, energizing in the good. Overcome evil with good. Resist evil and it will flee from you. So long as those you love are absorbed in the things that in the past have led you to worry over them, be tender and sympathetic with them, surround them with your holy and helpful love.

Jesus was tender and compassionate with all who were sick or diseased in body or mind. He was never angry with any, save the proud and self-righteous Pharisees. He tenderly forgave the adulterous woman, justified the publican and never lectured or rebuked those who came to have their bodily and mental infirmities removed by him. Let us then be tender with the erring and the sinful, rather than censorious, and full of rebuke. Is it not the better way to point out the right - overcome the evil with the good, and thus bind our erring loved ones more firmly to ourselves. Surely our own errors, failures, weaknesses and sins ought to have taught us this lesson.

In the bedroom of a friend where I recently slept, was a card on which was illuminated these words, which bear particularly upon this subject:

The life that has not known and accepted sorrow is strangely crude and untaught; it can neither help nor teach, for it has never learned. The life that has spurned the lesson of sorrow, or failed to read it aright, is cold and hard. But the life that has been disciplined by sorrow is courageous and full of holy and gentle love.

And it is this holy, gentle, and courageous love that we need to exercise every day towards those who require it, rather than the worry that frets still more, irritates, and widens the gulf already existent. So, reader, don't worry, but help, sympathetically and lovingly, and above all, don't become indifferent, hard-hearted and selfish.

CHAPTER XXV

WORRIES AND HOBBIES

Though these words are much alike in sound they have no sympathy one with another. Put them in active operation and they rush at each other's throats far worse than Allies and Germans are now fighting. They strive for a death grip, and as soon as one gets hold he hangs on to the end - if he can. Yet, as in all conflicts, the right is sure to win in an equal combat, the right of the hobby is absolutely certain to win over the wrong of the worry.

Webster defines a hobby as: "A subject or plan which one is constantly setting off," or "a favorite and ever recurring theme of discourse, thought, or effort," but the editor of *The Century Dictionary* has a better definition, more in accord with modern thought, viz., "That which a person persistently pursues or dwells upon with zeal or delight, as if riding a horse."

Are you cursed by the demon of worry? Has he got a death grip on your throat? Do you want to be freed from his throttling assaults? If so, get a hobby, the more mentally occupying the better, and ride it earnestly, sincerely, furiously. Let it be what it will, it will far more than pay in the end, when you find yourself free from the nightmare of worry that has so relentlessly ridden you for so long. Collect bugs, old china, Indian baskets, Indian blankets, pipes, domestic implements, war paraphanalia, photographs, butterflies; make an herbarium of the flowers of your State; collect postage stamps, old books, first editions; go in for extra-illustrating books; pick up and classify all the stray phrases you hear - do anything that will occupy your mind to the exclusion of worry.

And let me here add a thought - the more unselfish you can make your hobby the better it will be for you. Perhaps I can put it even in a better way yet: The less your hobby is entered into with the purely personal purpose of pleasing yourself, and the more actively you can make it beneficial, helpful, joy-giving to others, the more potent for good it will be in aiding you to get rid of your worries. He who blesses another is thrice blessed, for he not only blesses himself by the act, but brings upon himself the blessing of the recipient and of Almighty God, with the oft-added blessing of those who learn of the good deed and breathe a prayer of commendation for him. In San Francisco there is a newspaper man who writes in a quaint, peculiar, simple, yet subtle fashion, who signs himself "K.C.B." During the Panama-Pacific Exposition one of his hobbies was to plan to take there all the poor youngsters of the streets, the newsboys, the little ones in hospitals, the incurables, the down-and-outers of the work-house and poor-farm, and finally, the almost forgotten old men and women of the almshouses.

I saw strong men weep with deep emotion at the procession of automobiles conveying the happy though generally silent throngs on one of these occasions, and "K.C.B." must have felt the showers of blessings that were sent in his direction from those who saw and appreciated his beautiful helpfulness.

There is nothing to hinder any man, woman, youth or maiden from doing exactly the same kind of thing, with the same spirit, and bringing a few hours of happiness to the needy, thus driving worry out of the mind, putting it *hors de combat*, so that it need never again rise from the field.

Every blind asylum, children's hospital, slum, old lady's home, old man's home, almshouse, poor-farm, work-house, insane asylum, prison, and a thousand other centers where the poor, needy, sick and afflicted gather, has its lonely hearts that long for cherishing, aching brows that need to be soothed, pain to be alleviated; and there is no panacea so potent in removing the worries of our own life as to engage earnestly in removing the positive and active ills of others.

People occasionally ask me if I have any hobby that has helped me ward off the attacks of worry. I do not believe I have ever answered this question as fully as I might have done, so I will attempt to do so now. One of my first hobbies was food reform and hygienic living. When I was little more than twelve years of age I became a vegetarian and for nine years lived the life pretty rigorously. I have always believed that simpler, plainer living than most of us indulge in, more open air life, sleeping, working, living out of doors, more active, physical exercise of a useful character, would be beneficial. Then I became a student of memory culture. Professor William Stokes of the Royal Polytechnic Institution became my friend, and for years I studied his system of Mnemonics, or as it was generally termed "Artificial Memory." Then I taught it for a number of years, and evolved from it certain fundamental principles upon which I have largely based the cultivation of my own memory and mentality, and for which I can never be sufficiently thankful. Then I desired to be a public speaker. I became a "hobbyist" on pronunciation, enunciation, purity of voice, phrasing and getting the thought of my own mind in the best and quickest possible way into the minds of others. For years I kept a small book in which I jotted down every word, its derivation and full meaning with which I was not familiar. I studied clear enunciation by the hour; indeed as I walked through the streets I recited to myself, aloud, so that I could hear my own enunciation, such poems as Southey's *Cataract of Lodore*, where almost every word terminates in "ing." For I had heard many great English and American speakers whose failure to pronounce this terminal "ing" in such words as coming, going, etc., used to distress me considerably. Other exercises were the catches, such as "Peter Piper picks a peck of pickled peppers," or "Selina Seamstich stitches seven seams slowly, surely, serenely and slovenly," or "Around a rugged rock a ragged rascal ran a rural race." Then, too, Professor Stokes had composed a wonderful yarn about the memory, entitled "My M-made memory medley, mentioning memory's most marvelous manifestations." This took up as much as three or four pages of this book, every word beginning with m. It was a marvelous exercise for lingual development. He also had "The Far-Famed Fairy Tale of Fenella," and these were constantly and continuously recited, with scrupulous care as to enunciation. My father was an old-time conductor of choral and oratorio societies, and was the leader of a large choir. I had a good alto voice and under his wise dicipline it was cultivated, and I was a certificated reader of music at sight before I was ten years old. Then I taught myself to play the organ, and before I was twenty I was the organist and choir-master of one of the largest Congregational churches of my native town, having often helped my father in the past years to drill and conduct oratorios such as *The Messiah, Elijah, The Creation*, etc. When I began to speak in public the only special instruction I had for the cultivation of the voice was a few words from my father to this effect: Stand before the looking-glass and insist that your face appear pleasant and agreeable. Speak the sentence you wish to hear. Listen to your own voice, you can tell as well as anyone else whether its sound is nasal, harsh, raucous, disagreeable, affected, or in any way displeasing or unnatural. Insist upon a pure, clear, natural, pleasing tone, and that's all there is to it. When you appear before an audience speak to the persons at the further end of the hall and if they can hear you don't worry about anyone else. Later, when I had become fairly launched as a public speaker, he came to visit me, and when I appeared on my platform that night I found scattered around on the floor, where none could see them but myself, several placards upon which he had printed in easily-read capitals: Don't shout - keep cool. Avoid ranting. Make each point clear. Don't ramble, etc.

When I was about fourteen I took up phonography, or stenography as it is now known. This was an aid in reporting speeches, making notes, etc., but one of its greatest helps was in the matter of analysing the sounds of words thus aiding me in their clear enunciation.

At this time I was also a Sunday school teacher, and at

sixteen years of age, a local preacher in the Methodist church. This led to my becoming an active minister of that denomination after I came to the United States, and for seven years I was as active as I knew how to be in the discharge of this work. In my desire to make my preaching effective and helpful I studied unweariedly and took up astronomy, buying a three inch telescope, and soon became elected to Fellowship in the Royal Astronomical Society of England. Then I took up microscopy, buying the fine microscope from Dr. Dallinger, President of the Royal Microscopical Society, with which he had done his great work on bacilli - and which, by-the-way, was later stolen from me - and I was speedily elected a Fellow of that distinguished Society. A little later Joseph Le Conte, the beloved geologist of the California State University, took me under his wing, and set me to work solving problems in geology, and I was elected, in due time, a Fellow of the Geological Society of England, a society honored by the counsels of such men as Tyndall, Murchison, Lyell, and all the great geologists of the English speaking world.

Just before I left the ministry, in 1889, I took up, with a great deal of zeal, the study of the poet Browning. I had already yielded to the charm of Ruskin - whom I personally knew - and Carlyle, but Browning opened up a new world of elevated thought to me, in which I am still a happy dweller. In seeking a new vocation I naturally gravitated towards several lines of thought and study, all of which have influenced materially my later life, and all of which I pursued with the devotion accorded only to hobbies. These were I: A deeper study of Nature, in her larger and manifestations, as the Grand Canyon of Arizona, the Petrified Forest, the Yosemite Valley, the Big Trees, the High Sierras, (with their snow-clad summits, glaciers, lakes, canyons, forests, flora and fauna), the Colorado and Mohave Deserts, the Colorado River, the Painted Desert, and the many regions upon which I have written books. II: The social conditions of the submerged tenth, which led to my writing of a book on *The Dark Places of Chicago* which was the stimulating cause of W.T. Stead's soul-stirring book *If Christ Came to Chicago.* Here was and is the secret of my interest in all problems dealing with social unrest, the treatment of the poor and sinful, etc., for I was Chaplain for two years of two homes for unfortunate women and girls. III. A deeper study of the Indians, in whom I had always been interested, and which has led to my several books on the Indians themselves, their Basketry, Blanketry, etc. IV. A more detailed study of the literature of California and the West, and also, V. A more comprehensive study of the development of California and other western states, in order that I might lecture more acceptably upon these facinating themes.

Here, then, are some of the hobbies that have made, and are making, my life what it is. I leave it to my readers to determine which has been the better - to spend my hours, days, weeks, months and years in getting my livelihood and worrying, or in providing for my family and myself, and spending all the spare time I had upon these many and varied hobbies, some of which have developed into my life-work. And I sincerely hope I shall be absolved from any charge of either self-glorification or egotism in this recital of personal experiences. At the time I was passing through them I had no idea of their great value. They were the things to which something within me bade me flee to find refuge from the worries that were destroying me, and it is because of their triumphant success that I now recount them, in the fervent desire that they may bring hope to despondent souls, give courage to those who are now wavering, uncertain and pessimistic, and thus rid them of the demons of fret and worry.

Now that I have come to my final words where all my final admonitions should be placed, I find I have little left to say, I have said it all, reader, in the chapters you have read (or skipped.) Indeed I have not so much cared to preach to you myself, as to encourage, incite you to do your own preaching. This is, by far, the most effective, permanent and lasting. Improvement can come only from within. A seed of desire may be sown by an outsider, but it must grow in the soil of your soul, be harbored, sheltered, cared for, and finally beloved by your own very self, before it will flower into new life *for you*. That you may possess this new life - a life of work, of achievement, of usefulness to others - is my earnest desire, and this can come only to its fullest fruition in those who have learned to QUIT WORRYING.

Choose from Thousands of 1stWorldLibrary Classics By

Adolphus WilliamWard
Aesop
Agatha Christie
Alexander Aaronsohn
Alexander Kielland
Alexandre Dumas
Alfred Gatty
Alfred Ollivant
Alice Duer Miller
Alice Turner Curtis
Alice Dunbar
Ambrose Bierce
Amelia E. Barr
Andrew Lang
Andrew McFarland Davis
Anna Sewell
Annie Besant
Annie Hamilton Donnell
Annie Payson Call
Anton Chekhov
Arnold Bennett
Arthur Conan Doyle
Arthur Ransome
Atticus
B. M. Bower
Basil King
Bayard Taylor
Ben Macomber
Booth Tarkington
Bram Stoker
C. Collodi
C. E. Orr
C. M. Ingleby
Carolyn Wells
Catherine Parr Traill
Charles A. Eastman
Charles Dickens
Charles Dudley Warner
Charles Farrar Browne
Charles Ives
Charles Kingsley
Charles Lathrop Pack
Charles Whibley
Charles Willing Beale
Charlotte M. Braeme
Charlotte M.Yonge
Clair W. Hayes
Clarence Day Jr.
Clarence E. Mulford

Clemence Housman
Confucius
Cornelis DeWitt Wilcox
Cyril Burleigh
D. H. Lawrence
Daniel Defoe
David Garnett
Don Carlos Janes
Donald Keyhole
Dorothy Kilner
Dougan Clark
E. Nesbit
E.P.Roe
E. Phillips Oppenheim
Edgar Allan Poe
Edgar Rice Burroughs
Edith Wharton
Edward J. O'Biren
John Cournos
Edwin L. Arnold
Eleanor Atkins
Elizabeth Cleghorn
Gaskell
Elizabeth Von Arnim
Ellem Key
Emily Dickinson
Erasmus W. Jones
Ernie Howard Pie
Ethel Turner
Ethel Watts Mumford
Eugenie Foa
Eugene Wood
Evelyn Everett-Green
Everard Cotes
F. J. Cross
Federick Austin Ogg
Ferdinand Ossendowski
Francis Bacon
Francis Darwin
Frances Hodgson Burnett
Frank Gee Patchin
Frank Harris
Frank Jewett Mather
Frank L. Packard
Frederick Trevor Hill
Frederick Winslow Taylor
Friedrich Kerst
Friedrich Nietzsche
Fyodor Dostoyevsky

Gabrielle E. Jackson
Garrett P. Serviss
Gaston Leroux
George Ade
Geroge Bernard Shaw
George Ebers
George Eliot
George MacDonald
George Orwell
George Tucker
George W. Cable
George Wharton James
Gertrude Atherton
Grace E. King
Grant Allen
Guillermo A. Sherwell
Gulielma Zollinger
Gustav Flaubert
H. A. Cody
H. B. Irving
H. G. Wells
H. H. Munro
H. Irving Hancock
H. Rider Haggard
H. W. C. Davis
Hamilton Wright Mabie
Hans Christian Andersen
Harold Avery
Harold McGrath
Harriet Beecher Stowe
Harry Houidini
Helent Hunt Jackson
Helen Nicolay
Hendy David Thoreau
Henrik Ibsen
Henry Adams
Henry Ford
Henry Frost
Henry James
Henry Jones Ford
Henry Seton Merriman
Henry Wadsworth
Longfellow
Henry W Longfellow
Herbert A. Giles
Herbert N. Casson
Herman Hesse
Homer
Honore De Balzac

Horace Walpole
Horatio Alger, Jr.
Howard Pyle
Howard R. Garis
Hugh Lofting
Hugh Walpole
Humphry Ward
Ian Maclaren
Israel Abrahams
J.G.Austin
J. Henri Fabre
J. M. Barrie
J. Macdonald Oxley
J. S. Knowles
J. Storer Clouston
Jack London
Jacob Abbott
James Allen
James Lane Allen
James Andrews
James Baldwin
James DeMille
James Joyce
James Oliver Curwood
James Oppenheim
James Otis
Jane Austen
Jens Peter Jacobsen
Jerome K. Jerome
John Burroughs
John F. Kennedy
John Gay
John Glasworthy
John Habberton
John Joy Bell
John Milton
John Philip Sousa
Jonathan Swift
Joseph Carey
Joseph Conrad
Joseph Jacobs
Julian Hawthrone
Julies Vernes
Justin Huntly McCarthy
Kakuzo Okakura
Kenneth Grahame
Kate Langley Bosher
L. A. Abbot
L. T. Meade
L. Frank Baum
Laura Lee Hope

Laurence Housman
Leo Tolstoy
Leonid Andreyev
Lewis Carroll
Lilian Bell
Lloyd Osbourne
Louis Tracy
Louisa May Alcott
Lucy Fitch Perkins
Lucy Maud Montgomery
Lydia Miller Middleton
Lyndon Orr
M. H. Adams
Margaret E. Sangster
Margaret Vandercook
Maria Edgeworth
Maria Thompson Daviess
Mariano Azuela
Marion Polk Angellotti
Mark Overton
Mark Twain
Mary Austin
Mary Cole
Mary Rowlandson
Mary Wollstonecraft
Shelley
Max Beerbohm
Myra Kelly
Nathaniel Hawthrone
O. F. Walton
Oscar Wilde
Owen Johnson
P.G.Wodehouse
Paul and Mable Thorn
Paul G. Tomlinson
Paul Severing
Peter B. Kyne
Plato
R. Derby Holmes
R. L. Stevenson
Rabindranath Tagore
Rahul Alvares
Ralph Waldo Emmerson
Rene Descartes
Rex E. Beach
Richard Harding Davis
Richard Jefferies
Robert Barr
Robert Frost
Robert Gordon Anderson
Robert L. Drake

Robert Lansing
Robert Michael Ballantyne
Robert W. Chambers
Rosa Nouchette Carey
Ross Kay
Rudyard Kipling
Samuel B. Allison
Samuel Hopkins Adams
Sarah Bernhardt
Selma Lagerlof
Sherwood Anderson
Sigmund Freud
Standish O'Grady
Stanley Weyman
Stella Benson
Stephen Crane
Stewart Edward White
Stijn Streuvels
Swami Abhedananda
Swami Parmananda
T. S. Ackland
The Princess Der Ling
Thomas A. Janvier
Thomas A Kempis
Thomas Anderton
Thomas Bailey Aldrich
Thomas Bulfinch
Thomas De Quincey
Thomas H. Huxley
Thomas Hardy
Thomas More
Thornton W. Burgess
U. S. Grant
Valentine Williams
Victor Appleton
Virginia Woolf
Walter Scott
Washington Irving
Wilbur Lawton
Wilkie Collins
Willa Cather
Willard F. Baker
William Makepeace Thackeray
William W. Walter
Winston Churchill
Yei Theodora Ozaki
Young E. Allison
Zane Grey

www.ingramcontent.com/pod-product-compliance
Lightning Source LLC
Chambersburg PA
CBHW030010290326
41934CB00005B/291